LUCIER

FAMILY STORY

Volume One

LYDIA SIMMONS

Lydia Simmons
Editor In Chief

Shirley Starks Ali
David Reid
Christopher Starks
Executive Research &
Art Directors

Shirley Starks Ali
David Reid
Christopher Starks
Historians

Lydia Simmons
Curator

Condessa Uma
National Museum of African
American History and Culture
Curator

Patik Patel
Genealogy and Anthropology
Consultant

Sarah Allen
NARA
Consultant

Jamison Pandreas
NARA
Consultant

Jaunice Singleton
National Museum of African
American History and Culture
Consultant

Gunderson Dettmer
Legal and IP Counsel

PRESERVATION FOR FUTURE GENERATIONS
This book is the culmination of countless hours of dedication, collaboration, and meticulous effort by a team of individuals deeply committed to preserving and celebrating the rich history of the Lucier family. It stands as a living, comprehensive record and data set, carefully curated to ensure that the legacy of this remarkable family is documented, accessible and meaningful for future generations.

The journey to create this book began with a shared vision: to honor the Lucier family's history by weaving together stories, photographs, documents, and memories into a cohesive narrative. Achieving this required the expertise and passion of a diverse group of contributors, each playing a vital role in bringing this project to life. It is a testament to the power of collaboration and the importance of honoring our roots.

RESEARCH AND DOCUMENTATION
At the heart of this project was an extensive research process. Historians, genealogists, and family members worked tirelessly to uncover and verify historical records, ensuring the accuracy and depth of the information presented. From census records and birth certificates to personal letters and oral histories, every piece of data was meticulously examined and integrated into the book.

STORYTELLING AND NARRATIVE DEVELOPMENT
Writers and editors collaborated closely to transform raw data and fragmented stories into a compelling narrative. Their work involved crafting engaging prose and ensuring that the voices of family members were authentically represented. Through interviews and personal accounts, they captured the essence of the Lucier family's experiences, triumphs, and challenges.

VISUAL CURATION AND DESIGN
The visual elements of the book were curated with great care. Curators and historians worked together to select and restore photographs, documents, and other visual artifacts that bring the family's history to life. The layout and design of the book were thoughtfully planned to create an immersive and visually stunning experience for readers and to show our forward successes.

COLLABORATION AND COMMUNITY INVOLVEMENT
This project was truly a collaborative effort, involving professionals and members of the Lucier family along with their extended community. Family historians shared their knowledge, while younger generations contributed details about the most recent births. Their collective input ensured that the book reflects the family's complex story.

ACKNOWLEDGMENTS
This book would not have been possible without the dedication and hard work of everyone involved. Special thanks go to our historians, writers, editors, designers, and family members who contributed their time, expertise, and passion to this project. Their collective efforts have resulted in a work that documents the Lucier family's history and celebrates their enduring legacy.

In every page of this book, you will find the fingerprints of those who poured their hearts into its creation. It is a tribute to the past, a gift to the present, and a beacon for the future.

CONTENTS

DEDICATION 6
FOREWORD 7

CHAPTER 1 | NAME ORIGIN 8-14
Spelling and Pronunciation 10
First Recorded Name 11
Name Distribution 12
French Connection 12
General Living 13
Notables 13

CHAPTER 2 | WILLIAMSON, GA 15-31
Pike County Overview 17
Williamson Introduction 18
Georgia Militia District 19
History of Dark Town 20
County Homes 21
Landmarks 22-23
Williamson Businesses 24
Southern Railroad Company 25-26
Free Liberty Methodist Church 27-30

CHAPTER 3 | GREATS & GRANDS 32-76
Family Tree 34
Isaac Lesueur 35-38
Creek Muscogee Indian 38-39
Isaac Lesueur Jr. 40
Carter Lesueur 40
Henry Lesueur 40
Qualified Voters 41-42
Reconstruction Oath 42
Benjamin Lesueur 43-75
Scilla 43-75
William Beverley 43-49
Personal Property Taxes 51-55
Federal Census 57-60
Daniel Lucear 62
Fletcher Lucear 63-67
William & Eddie Lucear 66
Lucear WWII Service 67
William Lesueur 68-75
Benjamin Lucier 69-75

CHAPTER 4 | JOHN HENRY 77-92
Ludie Lucier 79-84
Chunn Family 80
William Lucier 83-84
Harriett Lucier 85-87
Thomas Lucier 86-87
Elnora Lucier 88-90
1900's Income & Expenditure 91

CHAPTER 5 | HENRY T. & ETHEL 93-136
Henry T. Lucier 95-133
Camp Gordon 97-102
WWI 97-105
92nd Infantry Division Gallery 106-122
Honorable Discharge 123-124
Central of Georgia Railway 125-127
Ethel Lindsey Lucier 128-135
Marriage License 130
VA Hospital 132
Tuskegee Airmen 133
Ethels Death 134

CHAPTER 6 | THE CHILDREN 137-178
James Henry Lucier 140-142
William Lucier 143-145
Catherine Lucier 146-148
Hermon Lucier 149-151
Sarah Lucier 152-154
Eleanor Lucier 155-157
Ben Lucier 158
Jeanette Lucier 159-161
Josephine Lucier 162-164
Josiah Lucier 165-170
Harold Lucier 171-173
Azzie Marshall 174-176

CHAPTER 7 | REUNIONS 179-1784
Lucier-Lindsey Reunion History 181-182
Pioneer Historian 183

CHAPTER 8 | GRANDCHILDREN 185-195
Generation Photo 187
Education 188-194
Civil Rights Movement 188-191
Scholars 192
Business Owners 193
Future Generations 194

CHAPTER 9 | MILITARY SERVICE 196-201

CHAPTER 10 | THE APPENDIX 202-216
Infographics 204-206
Glossary 207-208
Time Capsules 209-216

MEET THE AUTHOR & CHIEF EDITOR 217

DEDICATION

I hold on to a memory of a man in my dreams.

I didn't know him, but he knew me.

Then the next day, I'd see 3 or 4 more.

They just stood there wide eyed, left tokens,

and smiled by a door.

It's as if they were pointing me in the right direction.

They never spoke- their presence sent a message.

Last night, I hoped for them to visit again-

I've kept vigil for I knew we were kin.

Tonight, I will wait inside this warm dream

with a gift of honor, hope and peace.

Tomorrow, should they stop by once more for me;

may they hold true-

This, then, is for Thee.

Lydia Simmons

This book was created to honor the lives of
Henry Teasries Lucier and Ethel Lindsey Lucier.

NAME
ORIGIN

LUCIER

Lucier is a French surname that derives from the name Lussier.

LUCIER
French, French- Canadian Spelling

The usher's responsibilities include acting as the court bailiff, collecting fines and taxes; and overseeing the finances of the manors of the kingdom. The name was a title of nobility. The occupation can also be an official in the courts and prisons or a doorkeeper of the legislative chamber.

LUSIER
Italian Spelling

Lussier or Loussier is a surname of Italian origin. the name is an occupational name from Old French uissier 'usher', 'doorkeeper.' L'Huissier is a title of nobility given to the king's usher.

- **French/Italian Pronunciation: Loo-see-eh**
- **Our Pronunciation: Loo-see-er**

The name might have undergone spelling changes during the process of immigration or record-keeping in North America. Such variations in spelling were common due to factors like regional accents, literacy levels, and inconsistencies in record-keeping.

| **Lusher** | **Lasier** | **Lussier** | **Laseer** |
| **Lesuere** | **Lusear** | **Luzier** | **Lüscher** |

M.M. Lucier was one of the earliest recorded individuals with the Lucier surname to immigrate to the United States through Ellis Island, which had opened as an immigration station in 1892. He arrived in 1893 at the age of 21 aboard the Didam, a ship that departed from Amsterdam. While his full name was not documented at the Port of New York, his surname suggests a possible French or French-Canadian origin, as Lucier is commonly associated with those backgrounds.

Genealogical research and cross-referenced records indicate that variations of the Lucier surname existed in the U.S. prior to 1890, particularly in Georgia. We know that one primary lineage of the Lucier name was present in Georgia, but how our family came to exist and adopted the name remains elusive. This document will explore potential connections and origins of our surname, shedding light on its history and evolution.

1880			
Place	Incidence	Frequency	Rank in Area
🇺🇸 United States	271	1:185,309	16,412

In the year 1880, the United States records that the instance of a person being named "Lucier" or "Lusier" was 1 in 185,309 persons.

North America Distribution of Lucier's

Lucier families have moved over time throughout difference census years. The Lucier family name was found in the USA, the UK, Canada, and Scotland between 1840 and 1920. The most Lucier families were found in the USA in 1920. In 1880 there were 83 Lucier families living in New Hampshire. This was about 31% of all the recorded Lucier's in the USA. New Hampshire had the highest population of Lucier families in 1880.

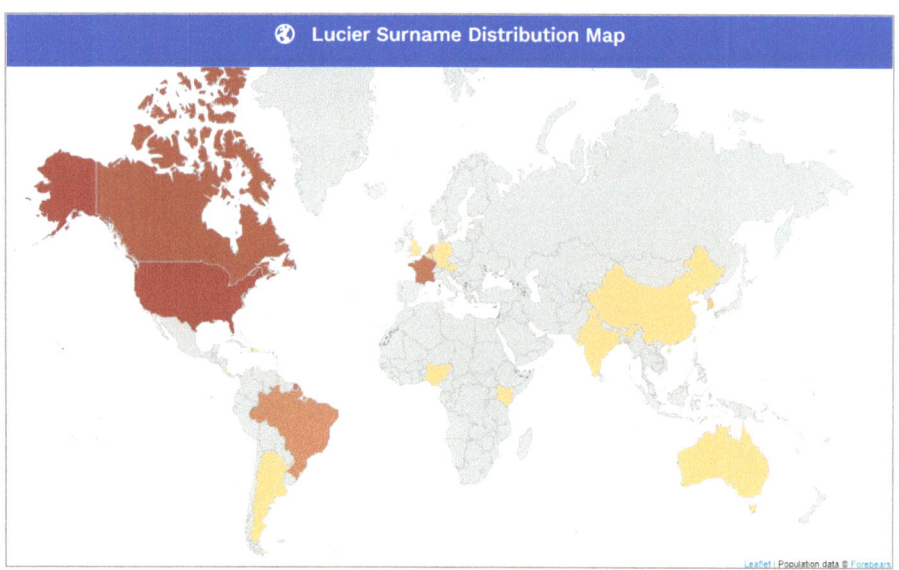

The French Connection

Lusiers are found in various parts of North America, particularly in areas with historical French or French-Canadian settlement. This includes Quebec, New England states, and other regions with significant French-Canadian immigration. The distribution of Lusiers would likely follow similar patterns to Luciers, influenced by historical French and French-Canadian migration.

Place	Incidence	Frequency	Rank in Area
United States	3,728	1:97,226	10,845
Canada	1,523	1:24,193	3,287
France	80	1:830,284	98,964
Brazil	16	1:13,379,646	256,605
Netherlands	12	1:1,407,265	75,423
Haiti	4	1:2,670,977	16,453
South Korea	3	1:17,080,085	2,793
England	2	1:27,859,030	389,889
Australia	1	1:26,995,701	270,794

In the year 2014, the United States recorded that the instance of a person being named "Lucier" or "Lusier" was 1 in 97,226 persons.

What did they do for a living?

In 1940, Laborer and Housekeeper were the top reported jobs for men and women in the USA named Lucier. 20% of Lucier men worked as a Laborer and 9% of Lucier women worked as a Housekeeper. Some less common occupations for Americans named Lucier were Salesman and Clerk.

Contemporary Notables of the name Lucier (post 1700)

Alvin Augustus Lucier Jr. (1931-2021), American composer of experimental music, professor at Wesleyan University in Middletown, Connecticut

James P. Lucier, American author, and was a staff member of the United States Senate

Wayne W. Lucier (b. 1979), former American football center

Louis Joseph Lucier (b. 1918), former American Major League Baseball pitcher

Mary Lucier (b. 1944), American artist

Étienne Lucier (1793-1853), American fur trader in what is now the Pacific Northwest

Alvin Lucier (b. 1931), American composer of experimental music and sound installations that explore acoustic phenomena

William Walter Lucier (b. 1868), American Republican politician, Member of Vermont State House of Representatives from Jay, 1910

Alvin J. Lucier, American politician, Member of New Hampshire State Senate 20th District, 1911-12

Alvin A. Lucier, American Democratic Party politician, Mayor of Nashua, New Hampshire, 1937; Member of Democratic National Committee from New Hampshire, 1939-40; Delegate to Democratic National Convention from New Hampshire, 1940

LUCIER

WILLIAMSON
GEORGIA

LUCIER

LUCIER

PIKE COUNTY, GEORGIA

In 1822 Pike County, the state's fifty-sixth county, was created from Monroe County in west central Georgia by the state legislature. Later, parts of Pike County were used to create Upson (1824), Spalding (1851), and Lamar (1920) counties.

Pike County, which comprises 218 square miles, and its county seat, Zebulon, are named after Zebulon Pike, a general in the War of 1812 (1812-15) and an explorer of the Louisiana Territory. Pike's name was made famous by his discovery of a Colorado mountain, subsequently named Pikes Peak.

Zebulon was incorporated in 1825, and a two-story wood-frame building was constructed to serve as a courthouse. This building served the county until 1844, when a brick building in the "Greek Temple" style replaced it. This structure was, in turn, replaced by the present courthouse in 1895. Other incorporated towns in Pike County are Concord, Meansville, Molena, and Williamson.

Early white settlers to the area used Indian trails in lieu of roads, but in the 1830s they improved the main trail by laying down planks that could support stagecoaches. This route became known as the Old Plank Road. Another old stagecoach line in Pike County came from Columbus, traversed Pike County up to Indian Springs, and then continued to Augusta. This was known as the Old Alabama Road.

Agricultural and forest products have traditionally been the economic mainstay in Pike County. Early crops were cotton and peaches. Later, poultry and soybeans became important farm products as well. Beginning in the 1970s, the county emerged as one of metropolitan Atlanta's bedroom communities.

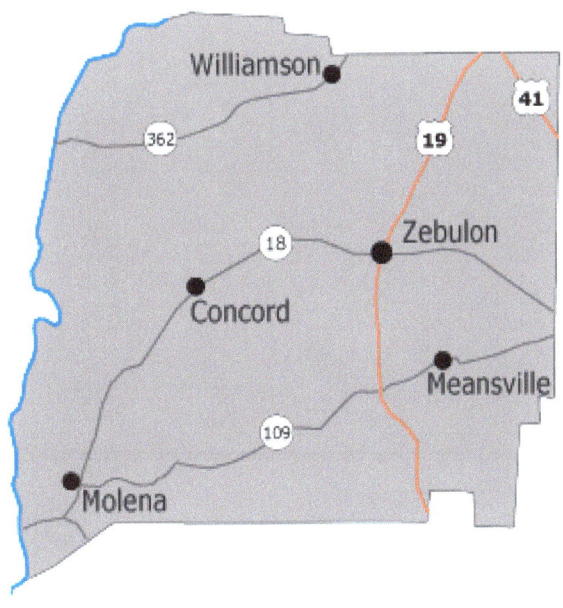

Williamson was originally known as Driver, for Mr. Giles [or Gillis] Driver, who ran an inn in the community. When Mr. Driver sold the inn to a Mr. Stearns, the area became known as Stearnsville. Later, Judge Ike Williamson (Slave Owner, Farmer and Money Lender) bought up thousands of acres of area land and when he gave land to the railroad for commerce, it finally became Williamson.

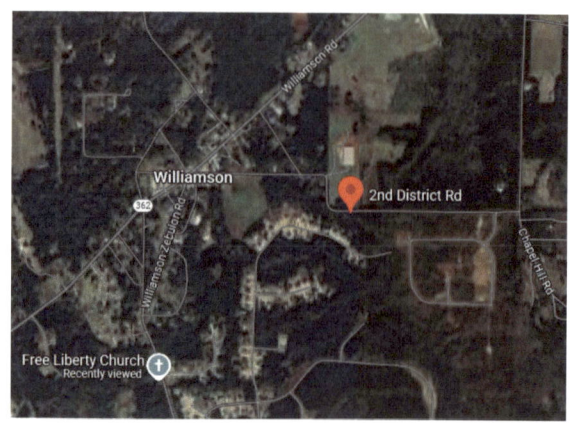

The Georgia General Assembly incorporated Williamson as a town on Agust 17, 1908. Williamson was incorporated as a city in 1970.

Williamson is located at 33°10'47"N 84°21'47"W (33.179743, -84.362976).

According to the United States Census Bureau, the town has a total area of 0.6 square miles (1.6 km2), all land.

As of the census of 2000, there were 297 people, 115 households, and 86 families residing in the town. By 2020, its population was 681.

Historical population		
Census	Pop.	%±
1910	179	—
1920	249	39.1%
1930	226	−9.2%
1940	217	−4.0%
1950	211	−2.8%
1960	215	1.9%
1970	284	32.1%
1980	250	−12.0%
1990	295	18.0%
2000	297	0.7%
2010	352	18.5%
2020	681	93.5%
U.S. Decennial Census[9]		

The organized Georgia Militia, which was prominent during the Revolutionary War, the War of 1812, and various Indian conflicts until 1840, no longer exists in its traditional form. It was gradually replaced by Volunteer organizations and eventually by the National Guard in 1916. Although early state codes contained provisions for the Georgia Militia, by 1910, all references to it as a military force were removed. Today, every citizen of Georgia between 17 and 45, not in the National Guard or other military force, is technically part of the unorganized Georgia Militia, though this is mainly to serve as a potential pool for the draft in emergencies.

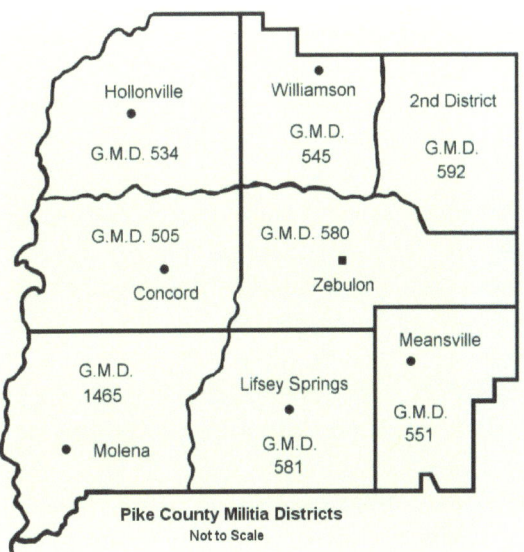

Pike County Militia Districts
Not to Scale

However, while the organized militia is defunct, the Georgia Militia Districts remain active and are important for several legal and administrative functions, such as determining the jurisdiction of Justice of the Peace Courts, election districts, property taxation, and land conveyance laws. These districts were historically linked to the captain in charge, with districts named after each captain, but they later became numbered through legislation passed in the early 1800s. Militia Districts have evolved over time, but they continue to play a key role in county governance, election procedures, and other local legal matters.

Within these militia districts are census "enumeration districts." So until the 1940 census is indexed by person, you will need to know approximately where your Pike ancestor lived, i.e., militia district and then enumeration district.

1930 E.D.	1940 E.D.	Description of Enumeration District
116-1	114-1	Militia District 505, Concord; Concord town
116-2	114-2	Militia District 505, Concord; that part outside Concord town
116-3	114-3	Militia District 534, Hollonville
116-4	114-4	Militia District 545, Williamson; Williamson town
116-5	114-5	Militia District 545, Williamson; that part outside Williamson town
116-6	114-6	Militia District 551, Meansville; Meansville town
116-7	114-7	Militia District 551, Meansville; that part outside Meansville town (Show separately Bethlehem Home for Children)
116-8	114-8	Militia District 580, Zebulon; Zebulon city
116-9	114-9	Militia District 580, Zebulon; that part outside Zebulon town (Show separately Pike County Jail, Pike County Poorhouse)
116-10	114-10	Militia District 581, Springs
116-11	114-11	Militia District 592, Second
116-12	114-12	Militia District 1465, Molena; Molena city
116-13	114-13	Militia District 1465, Molena; that part outside Molena city

How "Dark Town" got its name...

The town of Williamson, Georgia, historically referred to as "Darktown," offers a lens into the racial dynamics and social structures of the post-Civil War South. Dark town starts at Little Street and intersects at Second District Road; running East to Chapel Hill Road and West to Williamson- Zebulon Road (GA 362).

This nickname, shared by other predominantly African American communities across the region, reflects the intersection of racial identity, segregation, and the marginalization of Black residents during the late 19th and early 20th centuries. The term "Darktown" was not unique to Williamson; it appeared in various Southern states, including South Carolina, Alabama, and Mississippi, often used to describe areas where freedmen and their descendants settled after emancipation.

The origins of the nickname are deeply tied to the racial demographics of these communities. Following the Civil War, African Americans established independent towns and neighborhoods, seeking autonomy and safety in a society still grappling with the legacy of slavery. These areas, often populated entirely or predominantly by Black residents, became known colloquially as "Darktowns." The term was likely coined by white outsiders, including local officials, journalists, or residents, as a way to demarcate racial boundaries and reinforce the social hierarchies of the Jim Crow era. Its usage was not neutral; it carried a derogatory undertone, reflecting the pervasive racism of the time.

The negative connotations associated with the term "Darktown" were rooted in the stereotypes and prejudices of white society. It was often employed to imply that these communities were inferior, dangerous, or undesirable. This labeling was part of a broader pattern of systemic racism that sought to marginalize African Americans and maintain white supremacy. The term also appeared in popular culture, such as minstrel shows, where it was used to caricature and demean Black life, further embedding its derogatory meaning in the cultural consciousness.

Despite the negative implications of the nickname, the communities referred to as "Darktowns" were often vibrant centers of African American life. They were places where Black residents built schools, churches, and businesses, fostering resilience and solidarity in the face of systemic oppression. The story of Williamson, Georgia, and other "Darktowns" across the South is not just one of racial stigma but also of perseverance and community-building.

2nd District Road, Williamson, Georgia, 30292 | AKA "Dark Town"

Double-pen House

Blacks and Whites in Pike County and surrounding, in the early 1700 and 1800's (some even in the present day), lived in what is called "double-pen houses." These homes are of the saddlebag variety, with a central chimney, and the local areas were often surrounded by the kudzu plant.

Kudzu Plant

The Playhouse, a Christmas Shoppe

Jimmy's Food Mart

Original U.S. Postal Service

Williamson Train Depot

Williamson United Methodist Church

Announcement of the Depot removal

Free Liberty Methodist Church

Dr. Howards, Howard Connell's Store & Old Bank

Post Office

Businesses in Williamson, Georgia 1822-1922

Financial Business
The Bank of Williamson was incorporated in 1912, and the officers were I.B. Howard, President; C.A. Yarbrough, Vice-President; P.W. Vaughn, Cashier. Its Capital stock in 1912 was $25,000 USD.

General Business
- R.H. Yarbrough & Son, general merchandise
- Williamson Grocery Co., groceries and supplies
- W.S. Jackson, general merchandise
- R.H. McLucas, fancy and staple groceries
- B.A. Ridley, postmaster and dealer in cigars, tobaccos, stationery, etc.
- B.C. Wilson, auto tire shop and accessories
- F.L. Pitts, blacksmith and garage
- Williamson Bonded Warehouse, cotton storage
- Farmers Warehouse, cotton storage
- Hutchison and Vaughn, ginnery
- E.R. Reynolds, groceries
- Paul Beauchamp, cotton buyer
- A.P. Dickinson, nursery for raising peach trees

Medical Business
Three physicians: J.C. Beauchamp, I.B. Howard, and W.L. Beauchamp, who had recently opened up a baby hospital.

History of Pike County from 1822 to 1922
Rogers, R. W. | Library of Congress, Washington, DC

Between 1790 and 1970, Williamson, Georgia, was primarily an agricultural community, with cotton dominating as the main cash crop, especially in the 19th century. African American labor, both enslaved and later as sharecroppers or tenant farmers, was central to the cultivation and harvesting of cotton, as well as other crops like corn, tobacco, and vegetables. After emancipation, many Black families continued to work the land under exploitative systems, tending to crops such as cotton, corn, and peanuts, while also raising livestock and growing food for subsistence. By the mid-20th century, as agriculture modernized, soybeans and other diversified crops became more common, but Black labor remained integral to the region's farming economy throughout this period.

Southern Railroad Company

 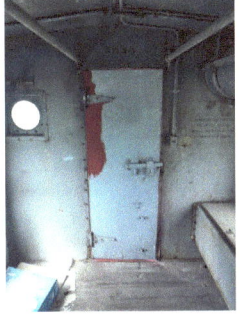  

   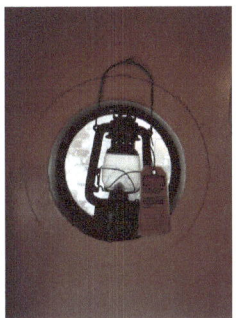

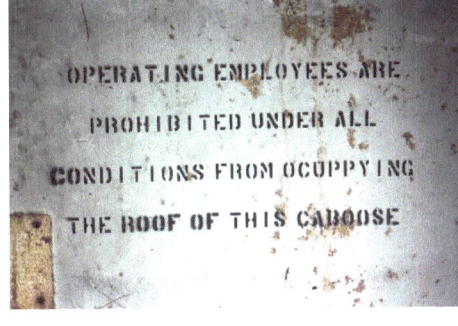

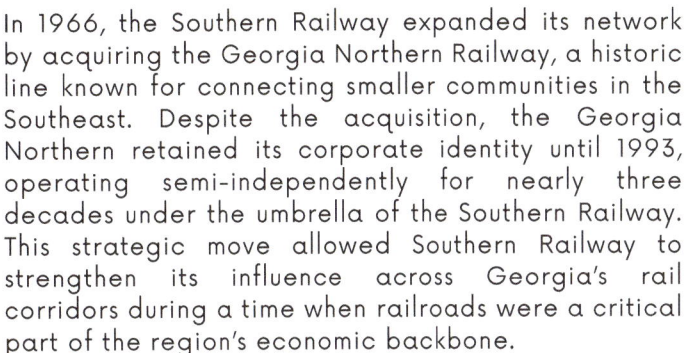

In 1966, the Southern Railway expanded its network by acquiring the Georgia Northern Railway, a historic line known for connecting smaller communities in the Southeast. Despite the acquisition, the Georgia Northern retained its corporate identity until 1993, operating semi-independently for nearly three decades under the umbrella of the Southern Railway. This strategic move allowed Southern Railway to strengthen its influence across Georgia's rail corridors during a time when railroads were a critical part of the region's economic backbone.

Williamson, Georgia, was a quintessential Southern Railway town, thriving in an era when railroads were the lifeline of small Southern communities. The town's strategic location made it a bustling junction where two key mainlines intersected: the Atlanta- Fort Valley line and the Atlanta- Columbus route. These lines connected rural areas to major urban centers, facilitating the transport of goods like cotton, timber, and other agricultural products that fueled the local economy.

As rail transportation declined in the late 20th century, so did the prominence of these lines. Both the Atlanta- Fort Valley and the Atlanta- Columbus routes were abandoned, victims of shifting transportation trends favoring highways and trucks. However, a small portion of the Atlanta-Columbus line still exists near Griffin, Georgia, serving as a faint echo of the region's railroad past.

Today, Williamson's railroads are a memory etched into the town's history, but their legacy remains a testament to the pivotal role the Southern Railway played in shaping Georgia's transportation and economy.

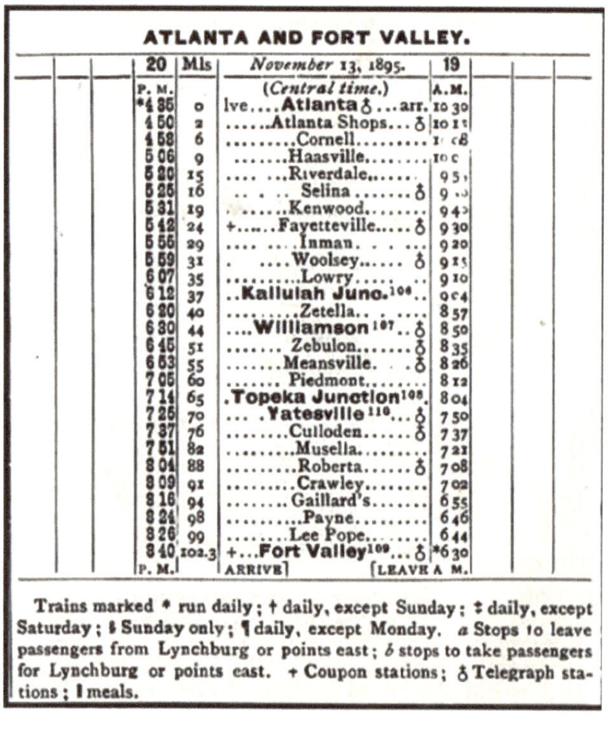

ATLANTA AND FORT VALLEY.			
20	Mls	*November 13, 1895.*	**19**
P.M.		(Central time.)	A.M.
*4 35	0	lve....**Atlanta** ♂...arr.	10 30
4 50	2	.....Atlanta Shops...♂	10 15
4 58	6	.....Cornell........	10 08
5 06	9	.....Haasville.......	10 0
5 22	15	.....Riverdale......	9 53
5 26	16	.....Selina......♂	9 40
5 31	19	.....Kenwood......	9 40
5 42	24	+....Fayetteville..♂	9 30
5 55	29	.....Inman........	9 20
5 59	31	.....Woolsey......	9 15
6 07	35	.....Lowry........	9 10
6 12	37	.**Kalluiah Junc**.106..	9 04
6 20	40	.....Zetella.......	8 57
6 30	44	..**Williamson**107..♂	8 50
6 45	51	.....Zebulon......♂	8 35
6 53	55	.....Meansville...♂	8 26
7 05	60	.....Piedmont.....	8 12
7 14	65	.**Topeka Junction**108.	8 04
7 25	70	..**Yatesville**110..♂	7 50
7 37	76	.....Culloden.....♂	7 37
7 51	82	.....Musella......♂	7 21
8 04	88	.....Roberta......♂	7 08
8 09	91	.....Crawley......	7 02
8 16	94	.....Gaillard's....	6 55
8 24	98	.....Payne.......	6 46
8 26	99	.....Lee Pope.....	6 44
8 40	102.3	+..**Fort Valley**109..♂	*6 30
P.M.		ARRIVE] [LEAVE	A.M.

Trains marked * run daily; † daily, except Sunday; ‡ daily, except Saturday; § Sunday only; ¶ daily, except Monday. *a* Stops to leave passengers from Lynchburg or points east; *b* stops to take passengers for Lynchburg or points east. + Coupon stations; ♂ Telegraph stations; ¶ meals.

Free Liberty Methodist Church established 1856

Free Liberty United Methodist Church (Free Liberty African Methodist Church before 1930), located at 1113 Zebulon-Williamson Road in Williamson, Georgia, was established in 1856 and has remained a cornerstone of faith, education, and community for generations. Like many churches of its time, Free Liberty served dual purposes- not only as a place of worship but also as a vital center for education and refuge for the Black community during and after slavery.

During the Reconstruction era, when Black children were barred from attending schools designated for white families, Free Liberty operated a schoolhouse to provide education for Black youth. These church-run schools were essential in empowering newly freed families, offering literacy and basic education despite systemic restrictions. With few resources and facing constant societal barriers, churches like Free Liberty played an instrumental role in uplifting the Black community.

"Legacy of Black Citizens of Pike County Georgia" Pike County Colored Schools refers to the school as "Unnamed school, 1899, teacher, Austin J. Reid; 20 males & 24 females"

Beyond its role in education, Free Liberty became a sanctuary for freedmen and their families, offering spiritual guidance, a place to organize, May Day celebrations, and a safe haven from racial violence and discrimination. The church also dedicated portions of its land as a burial site for Black members and their families, ensuring a final resting place at a time when segregation even extended to cemeteries.

village in giving showers for each bride and entertainments of every known variety. Flowers sent to sick and bereaved ones also.

In January, 1921, we became charter membrs of the Pike County Federation, and in October of the same year, members of the General Federation.

Our club house was formally dedicated and its doors thrown open to the public on April 30th, when with appropriate ceremonies, the cornerstone was laid by the Masonic fraternity. On the same day our club was hostess to the Pike County Federation at its first meeting.

A bulletin board, which has proved to be very useful, has been placed in the post office. We also conduct a second-hand magazine stand there, through the courtesy of the postmaster. At present, we are bending every effort toward beautifying the town well, for the benefit of the public at large, and as a memorial to one of our loved members.

Our membership is limited to twenty, and at prestnt we have ten active members. On our roll, however, are one in New York, one in Florida, two in Atlanta, one in Kenwood, and one in Zebulon, who pay their dues, thus testifying to the love that they still bear to the Woman's Club of Williamson.

COLORED CHURCHES AND SCHOOLS.

Up to the close of the Civil War in 1865, the colored people belonged to the same church as the whites and were served by the same pastors, holding their servies in the afternoons. In many of the Methodist churches, there were galleries built, and numbers of the servants occupied them during the services for white people. Some negroes were licensed as local preachers, and did much good among their own people, some of whom the writer remembers well, viz., Sandy Kendall and Edmund Lowe of Upson County, and

Wm. Fincher of Pike County.

Soon after the war the M. E. Church, South, organized the colored M. E. Church and has fostered it ever since. The other colored Methodists have gone either to the M. E. Church (North) or to the African M. E. Church. They have Methodist and Baptist churches at various places in the County, and have large memberships and enthusiastic services at all their churches. The A. M. E. Church in Zebulon has only 15 members. J. W. McKnight is the present pastor. The M. E. Church has 226 members and Jacob Maddox is pastor. The Baptist Church has 300 members and Monroe Watts is the present pastor. The M. E. Church for the colored people in Zebulon was organized 58 years ago. Jacob Maddox is also pastor at Meansville with 72 members, and at Roberts with 35 members.

The colored school in Zebulon has an enrollment of 186. There are schools and churches for colored people all over the county. They are noted for paying their pastors. The relations between the races are pleasant.

Floyd Slade runs an undertaker's establishment for colored people. Manuel Hall and Gilbert Baker run stores, and Robt. Lindsay and John Collier run blacksmith shops.

In cases of fire in Zebulon the colored people render valiant service.

Several colored soldiers died or were killed in France, but I have been unable to get the facts.

CONFEDERATE VETERANS.

In 1861, when Georgia seceded from the Union and took her place among the Confederate States of America, the call was made for troops to defend what we conceived to be our rights, as patriotic sons of the South our men and boys from 16 to 60 years arrayed themselves under the banner of the Confederacy and led by Jackson, Hood and

The church cemetery contains 227 memorials, with graves dating back to the early 1800s- before the church itself was formally established. These older graves suggest that the land had been used as a burial ground for Black individuals long before emancipation, possibly including enslaved persons and early freedmen. This deep historical connection to the land underscores the church's enduring role in preserving Black heritage in the region.

Free Liberty United Methodist Church remains a cherished cornerstone for the Lucier family, whose connection to its legacy spans generations. For the Black children of Williamson, Georgia, its walls once served as both a place of worship and a center for education. The church was also a proud participant in the All-Denominational Choir, a county-wide ensemble uniting voices from Black congregations across the area. Today, it continues to stand as a homecoming landmark, welcoming family and community members to gather in fellowship. With worship services held on the second and fourth Sundays of each month, Free Liberty's enduring spirit lives on, 169 years later, through faith, family and tradition.

Free Liberty is part of the North Georgia Conference of The United Methodist Church (NGUMC) and continues its mission of service and devotion.

LUCIER

GREATS
& GRANDS

LUCIER

HISTORICAL NAME VARIATION ADVISORY

In sections to follow, the names you will soon learn may have different spellings from year to year, census to census, and document to document. This discrepancy arises from the accuracy of the clerks recording the names and the reading and writing skills of the individuals listed. During the times many of these documents were created, recorders often prioritized other details over accuracy and struggled to interpret accents and dialects. Additionally, there was often little regard for the accurate recording of information about groups of people who were not considered human at that time. Take the time to follow the visual guides and examine the consistencies in the ledgers to understand how we traced and mapped our history, providing us with a clearer view of the past. Keep in mind that for every documented account of these individuals, there are likely thousands more whose stories may never be uncovered. For now, let us appreciate the knowledge of the past as we navigate our present.

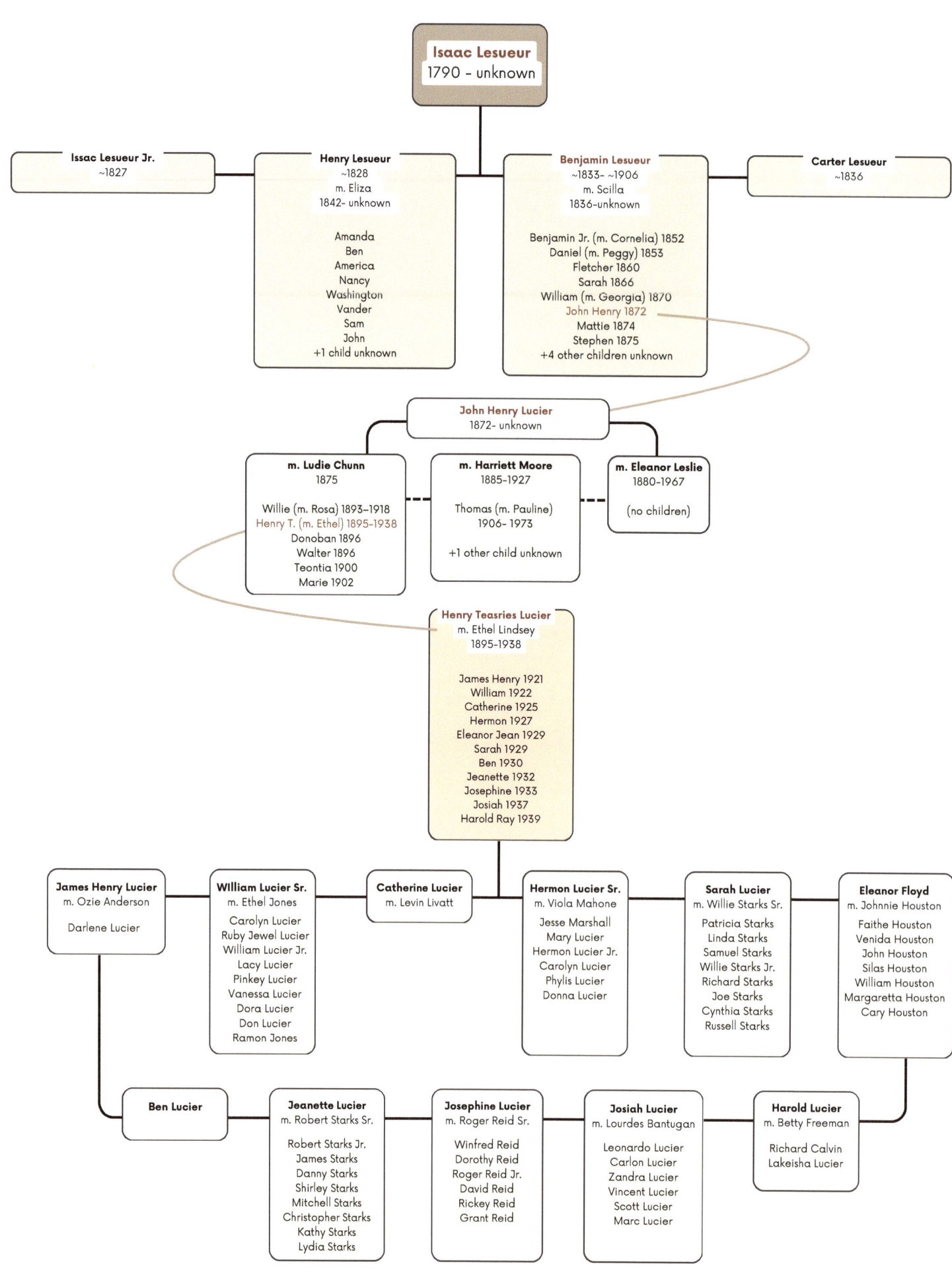

Isaac Lesueur (1790 - unknown)

The Earliest Known Chapter
The Lesueur family story begins with Isaac Lesueur, a man whose life straddled two starkly different worlds. Born in or about 1790, Isaac lived in Hollonville, Georgia (Militia District 534), during a time of profound upheaval and transition. Historical records reveal that Isaac was once an indentured servant, likely by William JH Taylor, a prominent landowner in the region. By the early 1800s, Isaac was listed in the status of a freedman, but this freedom was tenuous and burdened with systemic challenges. Heavy personal and estate taxes, likely exceeding his financial ability, left Isaac effectively bound in a system resembling slavery.

By 1836, Isaac had 4 sons: **Isaac Jr., Carter, Henry,** and **Benjamin**.

What makes Isaac's story even more complex and remarkable, however, are indications that he was not solely of African descent. Research suggests that Isaac was of Native American heritage, specifically Muscogee Creek Indian, originating from the northwestern territories of Georgia in the 1700s. This discovery opens a deeper chapter into Isaac's lineage, connecting his story to the Creek peoples, who were once a dominant force in the southeastern United States.

The Creek People: A Historical Context
The Creek Nation, known as the Muscogee, inhabited the southeastern region of North America long before European settlers arrived. By the 1700s, they had established a network of villages across Georgia, Alabama, and Florida, engaging in agriculture, trade, and governance. The Creek were known for their matrilineal society, strong kinship ties, and a confederation of towns that operated with relative autonomy under shared cultural and political practices.

The arrival of European settlers and the expansion of the American colonies brought devastating changes. Throughout the 1700s and early 1800s, the Creek people faced increasing encroachment on their lands, leading to conflicts such as the Creek War of 1813–1814. Many Creek were forcibly removed from their homelands, particularly after the passage of the Indian Removal Act of 1830. Others were captured during conflicts or raids, enslaved, and sold into servitude alongside African Americans. It was not uncommon for Native Americans like Isaac to be stripped of their identity and reclassified as "Colored" in legal and social systems, further erasing their Indigenous heritage.

Isaac's Connection to the Creek Story
While specific details of Isaac's early life remain elusive, his ties to the Creek people suggest that his journey into Pike County may have begun through these colonial conflicts and forced displacements. By the time Isaac appeared in records tied to Hollonville, he was on the plantation of William JH Taylor, but listed as a freedman. His relation to the county shows indentured servitude, which was a permanent placement for people during this time as Taylor, like many landowners in Pike County, relied heavily on enslaved labor to maintain the agricultural economy of the region.

Isaac's status as a freedman by the early 1800s may have been the result of manumission, self-purchase, or a shift in the ownership structure of Taylor's estate. Yet, even as a freedman, Isaac was far from free in the truest sense. Pike County in the 1790s was a rural, agrarian society where personal and estate taxes imposed on Black freedmen often kept them tethered to exploitative labor arrangements.

The Role of WJH Taylor
William JH Taylor, was a landowner in Pike County. While specific details about Taylor's life remain scarce, his position as a plantation owner underscores the power dynamics of the time. Enslaved and indentured individuals like Isaac were integral to the economic success of plantations, and their lives were deeply influenced by the decisions and actions of their enslavers. Even after achieving nominal freedom, Isaac's life was shaped by the lingering effects of this system, including taxes and laws designed to perpetuate economic dependence.

Later Years and Legacy
While the exact details of Isaac's later years remain unclear, his life laid the foundation for a remarkable family legacy. His sons carried forward his determination, navigating the challenges of life as freedmen in a society rife with systemic barriers. Isaac's story, marked by endurance and fortitude, reflects the broader struggles and triumphs of Native and African American families in the antebellum and post-Civil War South. Isaac's life, 300 years later being shown and recorded into history reflects his financial wealth among his peers and counterparts in history.

Personal Estate Tax Log | Militia District 534

Aucunville

NAMES OF EMPLOYER.	NAMES OF FREEDMEN.	Polls	No. of acres of Land	Number	District	Section	City or Town Property	All other Property	Aggregate value of Property	Value there during 18	Tax on Polls
J T Coleman	Rich Crowder	1									
"	Monroe Atkin	1									
"	Moses Wilder	1									
"	Manuel Thomas	1									
H C Thornton	Aubrey White	1									
"	Gilbert Fletcher	1									
B H Brown	Joseph Banks	1									
J M Taylor	Booker Stone	1									
"	George Shrower	1									
Green English	Willis Watley	1									
"	James Watley	1									
"	Jack Williams	1									
"	Henry Bareby	1									
"	Pete Collier	1									
J H M English	Green Crowder	1									
"	Henry English	1									
"	Dick English	1									
E White	Ben White	1									
"	Bob Foster	1									
"	Ben Yambrough	1									
"	Rose Swan	1									
"	Hardy English	1									
J A Williams	Wesley Hand	1									
"	Henry Williams	1									
"	Green Williams	1									
Wm Sutton	Jef Crawford	1									
Mrs T Hartsfield	Daniel Sharks	1									
S Godard	Frank Butler	1									
M J Fary	James Green	1									
	Dick Mays	1									
W T H Taylor	Isaac Fagner	1									
J M Gardner	Fannie Vaughn	1									
	Henry Mullins	1									
	Thomas Carter	1									
	Sidney Smithen	1									
Eliza Ball	Charles White	1									
	Hiram Vaughn	1									
	Albert Mays	1									
	Wesley Darden	1									
W F Darden	Luke Darden	1									
	Berry Williams	1									
	Felix Darden	1									
		42									

The Muscogee (Creek) People

The Muscogee (Creek) were not a single tribe or people but a loose confederation (or association) of tribes and chiefdoms. Because most spoke a variation of the Muscogee language, the Creeks were sometimes called Muscogees. There were two distinct groups. The Upper Muscogee (Creek) lived in towns and villages in the northern half of Alabama.

The Lower Muscogee (Creek)* lived in towns and villages in western Georgia, southern Alabama, and northern Florida. The remaining Muscogee (Creek) territory- including most of Georgia- was primarily used for hunting.

The Upper and Lower Muscogee (Creek) were different parts of the confederation. Another part of the confederation was a group of Lower Muscogee (Creek) in southern Georgia and Florida known as Seminoles.

The Muscogee (Creek) Confederation was organized around a political unit known as the chiefdom. This consisted of one or more towns or settlements governed by a chief, known as a mico, and a tribal council. One of the mico's most important jobs was to represent his people when dealing with other chiefdoms or when conducting treaties with settlers.

*The Muscogee (Creek) Confederation (1805- 1827) was surrounded by other American Indian tribes. The Chickasaws and Choctaws, not shown on this map, were in present-day Mississippi to the west of the Muscogee (Creek) people.

Conflicts Between Muscogee (Creek) and Settlers

During the Revolutionary War, some Muscogee (Creek) sided with the British, carrying on frontier raids against Whig settlements. After the war, Georgian settlers demanded that the Muscogee (Creek) give up some of their lands as a punishment, specifically the land between the Ogeechee and the Oconee Rivers. The Muscogee (Creek) were divided over what to do. The Lower Muscogee (Creek) agreed to turn over territory, but the Upper Muscogee (Creek), led by Chief Alexander McGillivray, refused.

Fighting between Chief McGillivray's followers and settlers on the border of the Creek Nation almost evolved into a full-scale war. Finally, in 1790, President George Washington invited Chief McGillivray to New York City, which was then the nation's capital. The Muscogee (Creek) leader was persuaded (and, perhaps, took payment) to cede Muscogee lands between the Ogeechee and Oconee Rivers in Georgia. The 34-year-old chief died from an illness three years later. His dream of a strong Muscogee (Creek) nation was dying, too.

The Black Native American descendants fighting for the right to belong

Descendants of enslaved members of the Muscogee (Creek) Nation have been in a decadeslong fight for recognition after they were told they could no longer call themselves members.

According to Article III, Section 4 of the Muscogee Creek Nation's constitution, "Full citizenship in The Muscogee (Creek) Nation shall be those persons and their lineal descendants whose blood quantum is one-quarter (1/4) or more Muscogee (Creek) Indian, hereinafter referred to as those of full citizenship. All Muscogee (Creek) Indians by blood who are less than one-quarter (1/4) Muscogee (Creek) Indian by blood shall be considered citizens and shall have all rights and entitlement as members of the Muscogee (Creek) Nation except the right to hold office."

About 24,000 Creek people were removed on the Trail of Tears, and by 1860, the Creek Nation held 1,600 people in bondage. Historians estimate that by 1861, 8,000 to 10,000 Black people were enslaved by various tribes in Indian Territory.

Slavery ended in the greater U.S. in 1865 but not in the Creek Nation until 1866. That year, the U.S. government signed a treaty, freeing the tribe's enslaved peoples, now "freedmen," and giving them the right to tribal citizenship.

Despite the treaty, the question of freedmen citizenship would be debated for a century and a half. In 1898, the U.S. government divided Creek lands and gave allotments to each tribal member. Aiding that process were the Dawes Rolls, which were created by the federal government to categorize Creek people by their blood quantum or as "freedmen," people who had been enslaved or were descended from the formerly enslaved.

But the Dawes system was flawed, and it created a false binary between "freedmen" and "blood" citizens. Members were placed on the rolls based on how they looked, whom they associated with and where they lived.

No matter their actual ancestry, light-skinned people could end up on the blood roll, while darker-skinned people were listed on the freedmen roll. "There are plenty of examples in all the tribes in which people in the same family are put on two different rolls.

For a long time, the rolls were a matter of historical documentation. The people designated as Creek Freedmen were full citizens of the Creek Nation- until 1979, when everything changed.

That year, the tribe voted for a new constitution, changing the requirements for tribal citizenship. It required blood ancestry to belong to the tribe, using the final "by blood" Dawes Roll as proof. From that point on, anyone who previously had membership as a result of freedmen ancestry was unenrolled.

This was a significant hit to previous Black members. In the 1960s and '70s, the Creek Nation began to receive millions of dollars in federal payments for historical violations of treaties dating to the 1800s, and it was beginning to restructure its government.

Around this time, many tribes, like the Creek, were seeking new ways to reinforce their sovereignty from the U.S. government and their nations' social identities. Changing the terms of citizenship was one way to tell a new story about themselves. From that point on, to be a member of the Creek Nation meant to be a by-blood citizen.

Isaac Lesueur Jr.

Isaac Jr. was the namesake of his father, Isaac and the eldest of 4 sons. We are not certain where Isaac was born but he was listed as 37 years old in 1867, making his birth the around the year of 1830. Records indicate that as of August 7, 1867, Isaac had lived in Pike County for 12 years and had moved to the county in 1855 at 28 years old. We do not know how Isaac Jr. lived nor died. But it is undeniable that he existed.

Carter Lesueur

Carter's life is partially documented. He was the youngest son of Issac Lesuer. He was listed as being born in 1833 and moved to Pike County in 1842 at 6 years old (but there are conflicting rolls that indicated Carter may have been 9 years when moving to Pike County). He had been in the county for 34 years (although records indicate 25 years) by 1867. Despite being a freedman and a registered voter, Carter's experiences highlight the stark inequalities faced by Black men even after emancipation. One record reveal that Carter was charged with refusing to return to his assigned housing area. He was arrested, found guilty, and sentenced to wear a ball and chain for 20 days. It's abundantly clear that there was an injustice that Carter could not find rest over and he would show his disdain by risking his wellbeing and possible life in search of something better. A freedman who needs to ask permission to leave a location, charged when he does so without permission and for refusing to return is in fact not a Free Man.

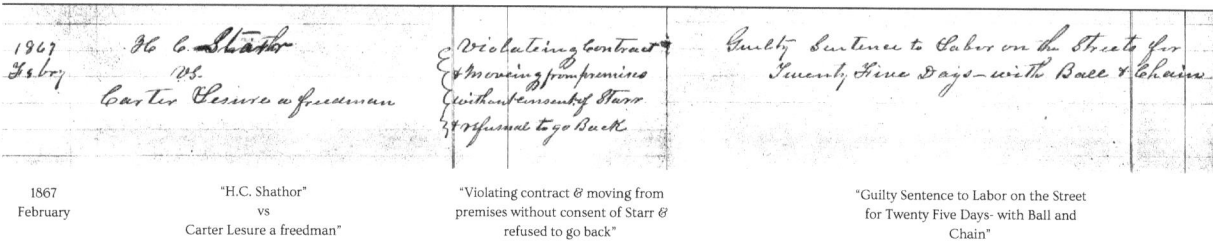

| 1867 February | "H.C. Shathor" vs Carter Lesure a freedman" | "Violating contract & moving from premises without consent of Starr & refused to go back" | "Guilty Sentence to Labor on the Street for Twenty Five Days- with Ball and Chain" |

Carter, his brothers, and their father were living in former slave housing and burdened by an ongoing debt of over ten dollars for the use of a "kitchen appliance." This debt, recorded on an official ledger filed with the courts, ensured that they could not leave the housing area except to work, after which they were required to return each night. This system of debt peonage, although slavery had been legally abolished, effectively perpetuated enslavement by other means. It reflects the harsh reality of life for freedmen in the Reconstruction-era South, where economic exploitation and legal loopholes undermined the promises of freedom. We do not know how Carter died nor the circumstances around his death.

Henry Lesueur

History details very little about Henry Lesuer. Records indicate that he was born in or about 1825 and had lived in Pike County for 18 years since 1849. He moved to the county at 18 years old. We are able to understand that at some point in 1897, he legally was allowed to marry Eliza (maiden name unknown) and had 8 children- **Amanda, Ben, America, Nancy, Washington, Vander, Sam,** and **John.** Records indicate that by 1870, Henry and Eliza relocated from Hollonville , Georgia (Militia District 534) to Barnesville, Georgia- once a part of Pike County, Georgia. By 1900 Henry and Eliza, now listed as being 75 and 58 years old lived at 3 Virgins Rons in Vineville, Georgia (Bibb County).

Georgia, U.S., Returns of Qualified Voters and Reconstruction Oath Books, 1867-1869

The "Returns of Qualified Voters and Reconstruction Oath" refers to documents and processes tied to the Reconstruction Era in U.S. history (1865–1877) following the Civil War. Specifically-
Returns of Qualified Voters.

These were records of individuals eligible to vote during Reconstruction. Eligibility often depended on meeting criteria set forth in Reconstruction Acts, such as taking loyalty oaths or demonstrating allegiance to the Union. Many Southern states were required to create new voter registration lists as part of the effort to re-establish civil government under Union guidelines. This often included newly enfranchised African American men and excluded some former Confederates.

Reconstruction Oath

Also known as a "loyalty oath," this was a declaration individuals had to swear or affirm to be considered loyal citizens of the United States.

The oath typically required individuals to renounce allegiance to the Confederacy and affirm support for the Constitution, laws of the United States, and Reconstruction policies. Taking the oath was often a prerequisite for voting, holding public office, or regaining property rights in former Confederate states.

The Reconstruction Oath and voter returns reflect the complex dynamics of restoring the Union and redefining civil rights and citizenship during this transformative period in American history.

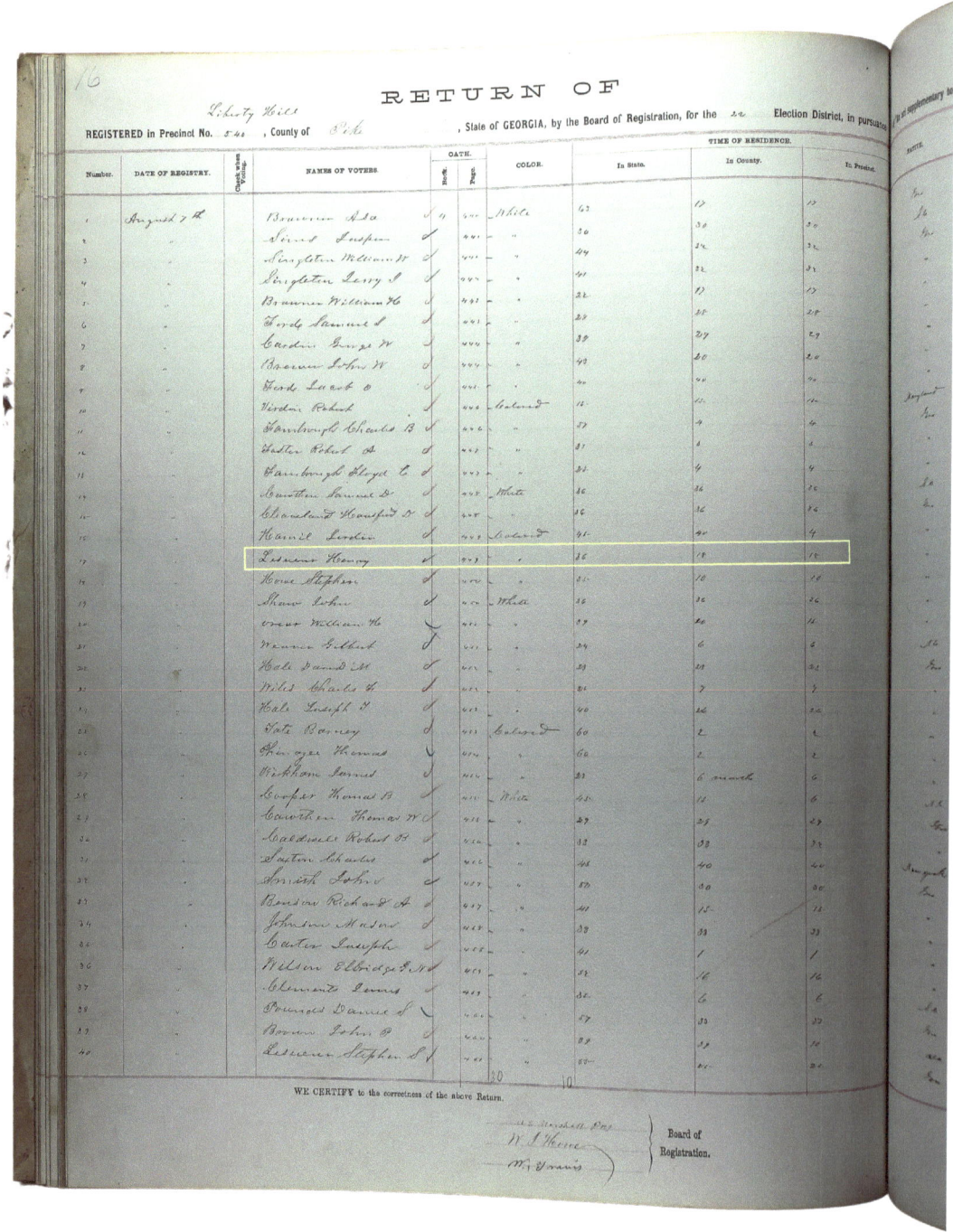

Benjamin Lesueur ~1830- (died between 1900 and 1910)

Benjamin Lesueur was recorded as born in or about 1830 and moved to Pike County, Georgia in 1842 at 9 years old. By August 7, 1867, he reportedly had lived in the county for 25 years. As a freedman he endured the oppressive conditions of the antebellum South. The abolition of slavery following the Civil War marked a significant turning point in his life, transitioning him into the uncertain role of freedman navigating the challenges of the Reconstruction era. He married Scilla (Last name often listed as "C." in historical and census records) though we are not certain, it appears that they married in or about 1870.

Scilla (Beverley) ~1833- unknown

Scilla Beverley's story profiles survival in the complex racial landscape of post-slavery America. Her origins are marked by an unusual and significant historical detail: her father and enslaver, William B. Beverley and mother, Delia signed for her, officially listing her mother's name, although listed as a slave. This act, rare for the time, suggests not only an acknowledgment of her birth but also a recognition of her legitimacy- an implication that carried profound social and legal weight in an era where the parentage of enslaved children was often disregarded or deliberately obscured. What's more notable is that although she was legitimized by her slaveholder and "father," it was not done for almost 20 years after her birth on September 26, 1856, according to the slave records of William B. Beverley. We therefore are left to deduce from what modern history has revealed about this era, that the abolishment of slavery prompted the move by her father. If true, the legitimation would likely ensure safety to Scilla among other predators that may have contemplated harm on her or her mother's life.

Notably, there are no documented passages detailing the arrival of Scilla or her mother into the United States on any of the registrar rolls. This absence raises a compelling possibility: Scilla's mother may not have been of African descent but instead belonged to one of the Native American tribes indigenous to Essex County, Virginia, during this period. The region was historically home to the Rappahannock, Pamunkey, and Mattaponi tribes, among others. If Scilla's mother was indeed Native American, her enslavement would reflect the often-overlooked reality that indigenous people were also subjected to bondage alongside Africans in colonial and early American history.

Upon the abolition of slavery, Scilla and her mother were freed, yet the circumstances that led her to Williamson remain unclear. One plausible explanation is that she was sold prior to emancipation and relocated. It was common for enslaved individuals from the Carolinas to be transported to Georgia, particularly Augusta and Elbert County- an area known as "Pike Town," named after General Albert Pike, a Confederate officer and Freemason who played a role in the migration of Southern settlers. Many families moved to Pike County in the mid-1800s, establishing farms and plantations under the belief that the county had been incorporated in honor of Pike's legacy.

Scilla's journey continued in the shifting racial dynamics of post-slavery Georgia. Classified as mulatto- a term used at the time to denote mixed African and European ancestry- she occupied a precarious space between racial identities. The end of slavery blurred, but did not erase, racial boundaries, and for lighter-skinned individuals like Scilla, the ability to "pass" as white became both an opportunity and a burden.

William Bradshaw Beverley
1791 - November 11, 1866

Background and Family Lineage
William B. Beverley belonged to a powerful Virginia family with deep colonial roots, one that played a key role in the early settlement and governance of the colony. Born in 1791 in Essex County, Virginia. William was the son of Robert and Jane Beverley and Brother of the infamous James Bradshaw Beverley. He was also the father of Scilla Beverley. The Beverley family first established itself in Virginia in the mid-1600s with Robert Beverley (circa 1635-1687), an English immigrant who quickly rose to prominence as a successful planter and politician.

Among his descendants, William Beverley (1696–1756), a significant and prominent colonial slaveholder and landowner, expanded the family's holdings by acquiring vast tracts of land, including Beverley Manor (now known as Cobble Hill Farm), a large area of over 118,000 acres in the Shenandoah Valley. The family's wealth and influence, passed down through generations, were largely built on the plantation economy and the institution of slavery. William B. Beverley, a descendant of this powerful lineage, inherited significant landholdings and social standing in Essex County, Virginia.

Land Ownership and Plantation Economy
Essex County, where William B. Beverley resided, was one of the many counties in Virginia where plantation agriculture flourished. The primary crop was tobacco, which required a substantial labor force. Like many elite planters in Virginia, the Beverleys relied on enslaved Africans to work their fields, manage domestic tasks, and perform skilled trades. The wealth and status of families like the Beverleys were inseparable from their use of enslaved labor.

William B. Beverley was one of the largest land owners in the state of Virginia and owned one or more plantations in Essex County, following the family's tradition of holding vast estates. These plantations were economic centers, with enslaved people forced to cultivate crops and manage various aspects of estate life. The family's affluence was directly tied to their large-scale exploitation of enslaved people, making them prominent members of Virginia's upper class.

Slaveholding Practices
The Beverley family's history, including that of William B. Beverley, is rooted in the systemic oppression of enslaved people. As a large landholder, Beverley owned many enslaved individuals, overseeing their labor in both agricultural and domestic capacities. It was common practice for slaveholders of his stature to be heavily involved in the buying, selling, and inheritance of enslaved people, a reality that dehumanized and commodified African Americans for generations.

Records from the period show that families like the Beverley's exercised absolute control over the lives of enslaved individuals, dictating their work schedules, living conditions, and even family arrangements. The system also often involved severe punishment for any perceived disobedience or attempt at rebellion. While specific records of William B. Beverley's practices may not be widely available, his role as a slaveholder fits within this broader context of exploitation and racial subjugation.

Social and Political Influence
As a wealthy landowner and a member of Virginia's planter class, William B. Beverley was a prominent figure in local governance and politics. He served in influential roles, such as justice of the peace and delegate in Virginia's General Assembly. The Beverley's, like many other elite families, shaped both the economic and political landscape of Essex County and beyond. They played a crucial role in maintaining the institution of slavery and advocating for the interests of the planter class.

Slave Registry | William B. Beverley
1856

REGISTER OF BIRTHS in the District of [the] ... Commissioner of [Essex] Records Essex Co. Va. during [with 1856] pages 1-4 are [bound with 1888 as preceding page 166]

REGISTER — 1856

Line	Date of Birth	Name of Child if Named	White	Free	Slave	Male	Female	Alive	Dead	Place of Birth	Father's Name in full if Child be free and born in wedlock, or Name of Owner if Child be born a Slave
1	Augt	Nancy			/		/	/		Essex County	Jno. W. Armstrong (for L.)
2	Decem. 10	Milton			/	/		/		"	Peter Ainsley
3	October	Georgiana			/		/	/		"	Do. Do.
4	March	Fanny			/		/	/		"	Tho. A. Boughton
5	January	William			/	/		/		"	Do. Do.
6	August	Unnamed			/		/	/		"	Do. Do.
7	August 26	Unnamed			/	/		/		"	Ann A. Dixide
8	October	Wm Thomas			/	/		/		"	Robert Brooks
9	Novem. 28	Georgiana			/		/	/		"	Jno. Washington Dowley
10	October 18	James Andrew			/	/		/		"	Jno. Franklin Dowley
11	March 20	Owen Franklin			/	/		/		"	Polly Dowley (for Life)
12	April 1	Charles & Harry			/	D	D	2	#	"	Wm. W. Brooke
13	Septem.	Lucy Ellen			/		/	/		"	Do. Do.
14	Septem.	Maria			/		/	/		"	Do. Do.
15	Septem.	Un Named			/		/	/		"	Do. Do.
16	October 4	Hugh Gwyn			/	/		/		"	Hugh Gwyn Billups
17	June	Robert Baylor			/	/		/		"	Robert Brooke
18	Novem. 2	Frances			/		/	/		"	Wm. B. Beverley
19	April 24	Stewart			/	/		/		"	Do. Do.
20	Feby. 20	Hyacinth			/	/		/		"	Do. Do.
21	Feby. 25	James			/	/		/		"	Do. Do.
22	Sept. 23	Scilla			/		/	/		"	Do. Do.
23	March 6	James			/	/		/		"	Jno. S. Fleming
24	April 25	Moseoo			/	/		/		"	Do. Do.
25	October	Betty Jane			/		/	/		"	Alvert W. Prudding
26	Feby. 5	Robert Faulconer			/	/		/		"	Richard Baylor
27	March	William			/	/		/		"	Do. Do.
28	July	Un Named			/		/	/		"	Wm. Breedlove
29	Octo. 9	Lewis & Henry			/	2		2		"	James Gray
30	March	Fanny Christian			/		/	/		"	

Beverley,	Anderson	John	Sarah Ann	Oct. 1859	King & Q.	52
"	Francis	Robert	------	Feb.27,1859	Spots.	45
"	James	James	------	Dec.20,1854	Spots.	12
"	James G.	Eugene	------	Aug. 1855	Spots.	13
"	"	John	------	Feb.20,1858	Spots.	35
"	Robert	(fem.)	------	May 1855	Fauquier	347
"	"	(fem.)	------	Aug. 1855	Fauquier	347
"	Robert E.	Elizabeth	Becky	Dec. 1856	Nottoway	28
"	"	Mary	Allis	Oct. 1856	Nottoway	28
"	Robert H.	Jno. Archer	Allis	May 19,1854	Nottoway	16
"	William B.	Austin	Kitty	--- --,1857	Essex	12
"	"	Brittan	Susan	May 7,1860	Essex	40
"	"	Edward	Charity	Feb.12,1860	Essex	40
"	"	Frances	Milley	Nov.27,1856	Essex	5
"	"	Frank	Britania	Jun.20,1857	Essex	12
"	"	Hyacinth	Sukey	Feb.20,1856	Essex	5
"	"	James	Mary	Feb.25,1856	Essex	5
"	"	Lewis	Caroline	Jul. 2,1857	Essex	12
"	"	Scilla	Delia	Sep.25,1856	Essex	5
"	"	Stephen	Charity	Jan. 1853	Essex	21
"	"	Stewart	Alice	Apr.24,1856	Essex	5
"	William G.	(fem.)	------	Aug.15,1855	Spots.	13
"	"	(fem.)	------	Aug.15,1856	Spots.	26
Beverly,	Robert	(?)	------	--- --,1856	Fauquier	363
"	"	(fem.)	------	Apr. 1853	Fauquier	387
"	"	(male)	------	Dec.30,1856	Fauquier	358
"	"	(male)	------	Feb. 1858	Fauquier	387
"	"	(male)	------	Jul. 1,1860	Fauquier	411

Cobble Hill Farm 1874

The land now known as Cobble Hill Farm was part of the original 1736 Manor of Beverley land grant and contained 188,491 acres. Between 1738- 1744, Colonel William Beverley of Essex County sold one quarter of this land, with an average acreage per farm of 503 acres. By 1760, three- quarters of the landowners in Beverley Manor owned between 100- 400 acres and by 1775 all of what had been forest in 1736 had become productive farmland.

The Confederates
Beverley, like many of his peers, lost everything (on paper) but emerged from the Civil War with his social position largely intact. Although the Southern economy and way of life had been irrevocably changed, men like Beverley were able to navigate the shifting political landscape to reclaim much of their pre- war influence. The 1865 pardon granted by President Andrew Johnson remains a significant marker of that moment in American history- when the country was forced to reconcile not only with the wounds of war but also with the deeply embedded inequalities that the conflict had sought to address.

Presidential Pardon of William B. Beverley
August 9, 1865

ANDREW JOHNSON,
PRESIDENT OF THE UNITED STATES OF AMERICA,

To all to whom these presents shall come, Greeting:

Whereas, William B. Beverley of Essex county, Virginia, by taking part in the late rebellion against the Government of the United States, has made himself liable to heavy pains and penalties;

And whereas, the circumstances of his case render him a proper object of Executive clemency:

Now, therefore, be it known, That I, ANDREW JOHNSON, President of the United States of America, in consideration of the premises, divers other good and sufficient reasons me thereunto moving, do hereby grant to the said William B. Beverley a full pardon and amnesty for all offences by him committed, arising from participation, direct or implied, in the said rebellion, conditioned as follows, viz: This pardon to begin and take effect from the day on which the said William B. Beverley shall take the oath prescribed in the Proclamation of the President, dated May 29, 1865; and to be void and of no effect if the said William B. Beverley shall hereafter, at any time, acquire any property whatever in slaves, or make use of slave labor; and that he first pay all costs which may have accrued in any proceedings hitherto instituted against his person or property:

And upon the further condition, That the said William B. Beverley shall notify the Secretary of State, in writing, that he has received and accepted the foregoing pardon.

In testimony whereof, I have hereunto signed my name and caused the Seal of the United States to be affixed.

Done at the CITY OF WASHINGTON, this Ninth day of August, A. D. 1865, and of the Independence of the United States the Ninetieth.

Andrew Johnson

By the President:
William H. Seward
Secretary of State.

President Andrew Johnson

As Johnson assumed the presidency, his attitude toward Confederate leaders seemed to signify punishment and prosecution for the rebellion. Many southern leaders fled the United States, going to Mexico, Canada, Europe and other countries. He doubled the number of exempted classes that had been exempted by Lincoln. Johnson's proclamation of May 29, 1865, for example, did not include anyone whose personal property exceeded $20,000 USD (equivalent to $398,000 USD in 2024). Several mitigating factors however led Johnson to greater clemency, such as the attitude of Lincoln for reconciliation and William H. Seward's similar leniency towards the former rebels.

"President Andrew Johnson Pardoning Rebels at the White House", Harper's Weekly, October 14, 1865
Those excluded from general amnesty had the option of applying to the president for a special pardon, and much of Johnson's time was spent in granting those pardons.

There were 12,652 pardons issued by June 5, 1866. Under Johnson's "thirteenth" exemption the number of pardons was issued in this order: Virginia, 2,070; Alabama, 1,361; Georgia 1,228; Mississippi, 765; South Carolina, 638; North Carolina, 482; Texas, 269; Louisiana, 142; Tennessee, 93; Arkansas, 41; West Virginia, 39; Florida, 22; Kentucky, 11; Missouri, 10.

William B. Beverley was a Confederate supporter during the American Civil War, likely serving either as a soldier or an active sympathizer of the Confederacy. His involvement in the Confederacy made him subject to penalties after the South's defeat. In 1865, he was pardoned by President Andrew Johnson, as part of the post-war reconciliation efforts. This pardon restored the legal rights of former Confederates, including the ability to own property and engage in political and civic life, reflecting Beverley's place among Southern elites who sought to rebuild their status during Reconstruction.

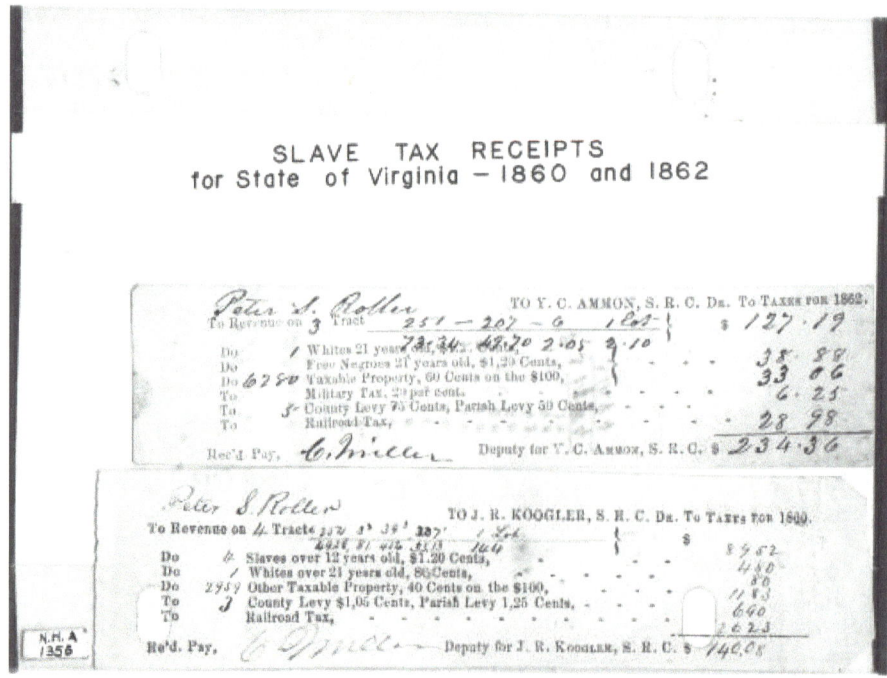

The Skin Advantage

Scilla's fair complexion likely allowed her access to spaces and privileges that were otherwise denied to her African American peers, yet it also required secrecy and constant vigilance. Passing as white provided Scilla with choices that would have otherwise been unavailable- such as legal marriage to a white man- but it also exposed her to the contradictions of a society that both favored and resented those of mixed heritage. Mulattos were often regarded as property of the white race when compared to Black individuals, yet they were simultaneously shunned for embodying the unspoken truth of white men's desire for and exploitation of Black and Indigenous women.

Male and Female "Mulatto" Children
The law binding out the children of white women by men of African descent until the age of thirty- one applied to their daughters and granddaughters as well. The law had a far greater impact on females than males. When men completed their indentures, they had the skills needed to earn a living in a trade or as farmers- even if some of their most productive years were behind them. Women who were bound out until thirty- one were likely to have children during their indenture. Each child added another five years to their service, in many cases making them servants for life and tying them to the slave population.

Marriage and Family Life
Despite the risks, Scilla chose a different path. She married Benjamin, a Black man who was Indigenous and listed on many records as "mulatto" as well; a decision that effectively marked her public identity as Black. In a world where race dictated one's social standing, her marriage meant the loss of any privileges that passing might have afforded her. Society's tolerance for racial ambiguity often ended when a person's allegiances were made clear, and for Scilla, choosing to love a Black man meant facing the full weight of discrimination. To some, she was a "nigger lover," an object of scorn and betrayal among those who might have otherwise accepted her if she had remained within the boundaries of whiteness.

Each time Scilla was found in historical accounts, her name was spelled differently. It was found as "Silla," "Cilla," "Zilla," and often "Silla C." After finding her slave registration and confirming through multiple cross registries, it is our belief that she had likely been communicating that her name was Scilla with a C. and the translation of that was typically shown as "Silla C." Scilla was documented on each census report as being unable to read nor write English. By 1900, census records indicate that Scilla was now going by the name "Luscilla." She and Benjamin was married approximately 30 years, suggesting their union began around 1870. Together, they had twelve children, though only eight survived into the 20th century: **Ben Jr. "Benji", Daniel, Fletcher, Sarah, William, Mattie, Stephen,** and **John Henry**. Their large family became a cornerstone of Benjamin's post-emancipation life, and living in Hollonville, Georgia was a constant reminder of oppression.

Enslaved Mulatto's vs Free Mulatto's in the 1800's

Freedman Tax Record & Employer
Hollonville, Georgia | 1878-1883

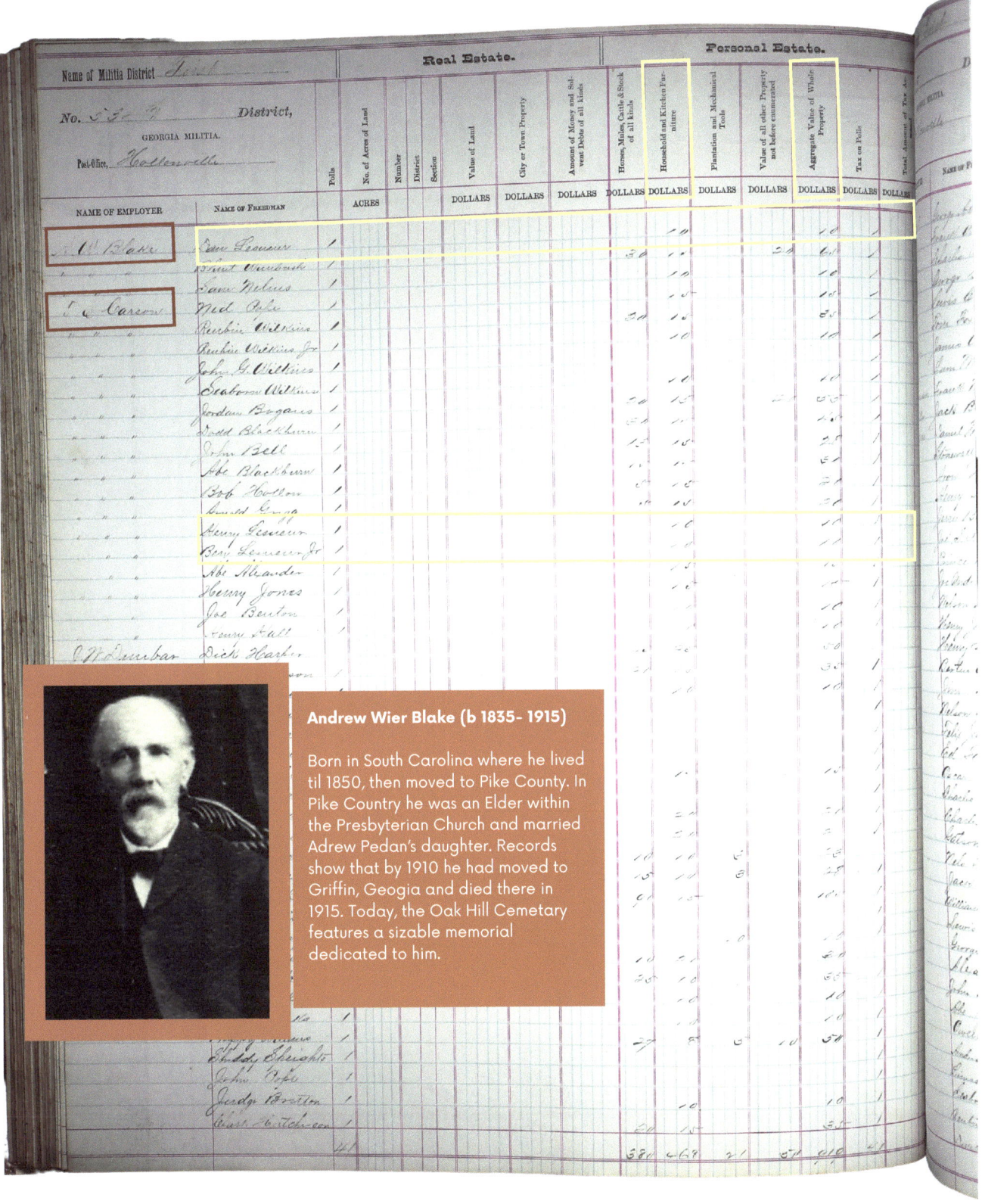

Andrew Wier Blake (b 1835- 1915)

Born in South Carolina where he lived til 1850, then moved to Pike County. In Pike Country he was an Elder within the Presbyterian Church and married Adrew Pedan's daughter. Records show that by 1910 he had moved to Griffin, Geogia and died there in 1915. Today, the Oak Hill Cemetary features a sizable memorial dedicated to him.

Employer: AW Blake | Dan Lesueur
Employer: TE Carson | John Henry, Ben "Benji" Lesueur Jr.

Tax Registry: Henry and Ben Lesueur | 1860s

Discriminatory Taxation
They suffered under the discriminatory Georgia tax law enacted in 1723 and restated in 1749 which described "Taxables" as:

All and every White Person, Male, of the Age of Sixteen Years, and upwards, all Negroes, Mulattoes, Mustees Male or Female, and all Persons of Mixt Blood, to the Fourth Generation, of the Age of Twelve Years, and upwards, and all white Persons intermarrying with any Negro, mulatto, or Mustee, or other Person of mixt Blood,...shall be deemed Taxables...
[Clark, State Records of Georgia, XXIII:106-7, 345].

Thus, free African American and Indian households can be identified by the taxation of their female family members over twelve years of age. Some light-skinned people would claim to be white to avoid this discriminatory tax, and they would be listed by the tax collector with the notation, "Refuses to list his wife." It was in the interest of the tax collector to classify those of doubtful ancestry as "Mulatto" since he received a portion of the tax. However, those with some political and economic influence like were often listed as white.

Indentured Apprenticeship
In addition to the discriminatory tax, poor and orphaned African American children were bound out until the age of twenty-one by the county courts just like their poor white counterparts.

Henry Lesueur, Ben Lesueur

Tax Record & Employer | June 16, 1864

Andrew Gilliland Peden (1811 – 1896)

FRIENDSHIP PRESBYTERIAN CHURCH
In 1849 Rev. Andrew G. Peden became pastor and served for twenty years. He was succeeded by Rev. L. H. Wilson, who was pastor for three years. Rev. Peden then resumed the pastorate and held it until his death in 1896.

Employer: HG Peden | Ben Lesueur

Tax Record & Employer

Name of Employer	Name of Freedman	Polls	Acres			Value of Land	City or Town Property	Amount of Money and Solvent Debts of all kinds	Horses, Mules, Cattle & Stock of all kinds	Household and Kitchen Furniture	Plantation and Mechanical Tools	Value of all other Property not before enumerated	Aggregate Value of Whole Property	Tax on Polls
A W Blake	Dan Lesueur	1								10			10	
"	Blunt Hurlock	1							30	10		20	60	1
"	Sam Nelms	1								10			10	
T E Carson	Ned Cole	1								10			10	
"	Reubin Wilkins	1							30	15			45	
"	Reubin Wilkins Jr	1								10			10	
"	John G Wilkins	1												
"	Seaborn Wilkins	1								10			10	
"	Jordan Bogans	1							20	15		20	55	1
"	Todd Blackburn	1							30				40	
"	John Bell	1							15	15			30	
"	Abe Blackburn	1								15			15	
"	Bob Hollow	1							10				20	
"	Arnold Gingo	1							10	10			20	
"	Henry Lesueur	1								10			10	
"	Ben Lesueur Jr	1								10			10	
"	Abe Alexander	1								15				
"	Henry Jones	1								10			10	
"	Joe Benton	1												
"	Henry Hall	1												
J M Dunbar	Dick Harper	1							20				30	
"	Frank Johnson	1							20				35	
Jue Coggin	Elijah Jones	1								10			10	
"	Wesley Adams	1												
J W Hood	John Peden	1												
"	Yancey Peden	1												
W Owen	Willis Cole	1								15			15	
M S Scott	William Jones	1												
M L Gaulding	Green Cross	1								20			20	
"	Mardy Hollow	1								20			20	
"	Mingo Harris	1							10	10	5		25	
"	Isaac Harris	1							15	10	5		25	
"	Wash Dewberry	1							60	15			100	
"	Felix Harris	1												
"	Andrew Jones	1								10				
"	Valentine Hood	1							10	20			30	
L Banks	Jack Griffin	1							30	10			65	
"	West Banks	1								10			10	
"	Jim Banks	1								10			10	
"	Neppy Adams	1							27	8	6	10	50	1
"	Shaddy Sheights	1												
"	John Cole	1												
"	Jordy Benton	1								10			10	
"	Mark Kitchen	1							20	10			30	
		41							581	269	21	60	919	

Employer: TE Carson | Henry Lesueur, Ben Lesueur Jr.

____ DISTRICT, GEORGIA MILITIA.

NAMES OF EMPLOYER.	NAMES OF FREEDMEN.	Polls.	Real Estate - No. of acres of Land.	Number.	District.	Section.	City or Town Property. DOLLARS.	All other Property. DOLLARS.	Aggregate value of Property. DOLLARS.	Value after deducting $200. DOLLARS.	Tax on Polls. DOLLARS.	Total am'nt of Tax Assessed. DOLLARS.
T. Anderson	Amos Lynch	1									1 60	
	Riley Hamilton	1									1 00	
Grey Dunn	Jno. Hancock	1									1 00	
	Jerry Beakham	1									1 00	
	Jes Chapman	1									1 00	
	Frank Williams	1									1 00	
Grey Dunn	Geo Dickinson	1									1 00	
	Willis Anderson	1									1 00	
	Mon Reid	1									1 00	
	Bill Dickinson	1									1 00	
	Henry Wiggins	1									1 00	
	Mose Baker	1									1 00	
W. Dunbar	Dick Harper	1									1 00	
	Jno. Bailey	1									1 00	
	Joe Madden	1									1 00	
Pink Holland	Frank Johnston	1									1 00	
	Randal Holland	1									1 00	
	Jim Haygood	1									1 00	
	Chas Westmoreland	1									1 00	
D. A. Adams	George Adams	1									1 00	
	Henry Williams	1									1 00	
CC Hood	Valentine Hood	1									1 00	
	George Hood	1									1 00	
	Charles Westmoreland	1									1 00	
	Andy Jones	1									1 00	
	Randal Holland	1									1 00	
JJ Irvin	Henry Irvin	1									1 00	
JE Turner	Sinken Huff	1									1 00	
JA Williams	Archy Williams	1									1 00	
	Wright Jackson	1									1 00	
Rd McDowell	Mitchell Parker	1									1 00	
	Edmund Alexander	1									1 00	
GE Dupree	Charles Moreland	1									1 00	
	Sam Moreland	1									1 00	
JE Carson	Dodson Blackburn	1									1 00	
	Ben Lesuer	1									1 00	
JW Blake	Ners Alexander	1									1 00	
	Abram Young	1									1 00	
CR Wilson	Alex Allen	1									1 00	
	Jasper Moreland	1									1 00	
	Robert Lasseter	1									1 00	
	Anthony Lasseter	1									1 00	
	Jesse Allen	1									1 00	
	Clay Williams		44								44 00	

In the 1860s, freedmen in Militia District 534, Georgia, were taxed as part of broader Reconstruction efforts to rebuild local economies and governments. However, these taxes often served as tools of economic control, closely tied to a system of indentured servitude. Local authorities imposed taxes, such as poll taxes and occupational fees, disproportionately on freedmen, deliberately creating financial burdens that limited their economic mobility. Many freedmen, unable to pay these taxes, were forced into exploitative labor arrangements like sharecropping or tenant farming to settle their debts. This taxation system effectively perpetuated a cycle of dependency and labor exploitation, undermining the freedoms promised by emancipation and reinforcing the racial hierarchy of the pre-war South.

an 1800's Farmhouse in Williamson, Pike, Georgia

A boy on an oxcart in 1890 in Pike County, Georgia USA

Federal Census:
County of Pike | July 7, 1870

		Name	Age	Sex	Color	Profession	Value Real Estate	Value Personal	Place of Birth										
1		Williams Howard	1	M	B				Georgia										
2		Chunn Mary J.	10	F	B	At Home			Georgia							1	1		
3	537 539	Chatman George	30	M	B	Farm Laborer			Georgia							1	1		1
4		— Mary	28	F	B	Keeping house			Georgia										
5		— Cilla	8	F	B				Georgia										
6		— Sarah	3	F	B				Georgia										
7		— George	1	M	B				Georgia										
8		Chatfield Lizzie	8	F	B				Georgia										
9	538 540	Bell George	28	M	B	Farm Laborer			Georgia							1	1		
10		— Amanda	24	F	B	Farm Laborer			Georgia							1	1		
11		Flemister Isaac	7	M	B				Georgia										
12	539 541	O'Neal Newton	26	M	W	Farmer	500	250	Georgia					Dec					1
13		— Anne	18	F	W	Keeping house			Georgia					Dec					
14	540 542	Adkins John	70	M	B	Farm Laborer			Virginia							1	1		
15		— Anne	69	F	B	Keeping house			Maryland							1	1		
16	541 543	Darden Isaac	40	M	B	Farm Laborer			Georgia							1	1		1
17		— Susan	35	F	B	Farm Laborer			Georgia							1	1		
18		— Georgia A.	18	F	B	Farm Laborer			Georgia							1	1		
19		— Branch	16	M	B	Farm Laborer			Georgia							1	1		
20		— Lewis	10	M	B	At home			Georgia							1	1		
21		— Paul	8	M	B				Georgia										
22		— Lydia	6	F	B				Georgia										
23		— Fanny	9/12	F	B				Georgia					Nov					
24	542 544	Secures Benjamin	40	M	B	Farm Laborer			Georgia							1	1		1
25		— Cilla	38	F	B	Farm Laborer			Virginia							1	1		
26		— Daniel	17	M	B	Farm Laborer			Georgia							1	1		
27		— Fletcher	10	M	B	At home			Georgia							1	1		
28		— Stephen	8	M	B				Georgia										
29		— Mattie	6	F	B				Georgia										
30		— Sarah	4	F	B				Georgia										
31		— Henry	9/12	M	B				Georgia					Nov					

Benjamin, Scilla, Daniel, Fletcher, Stephen, Mattie, Sarah, John Henry

Federal Census:
County of Pike, Georgia | June 11, 1880

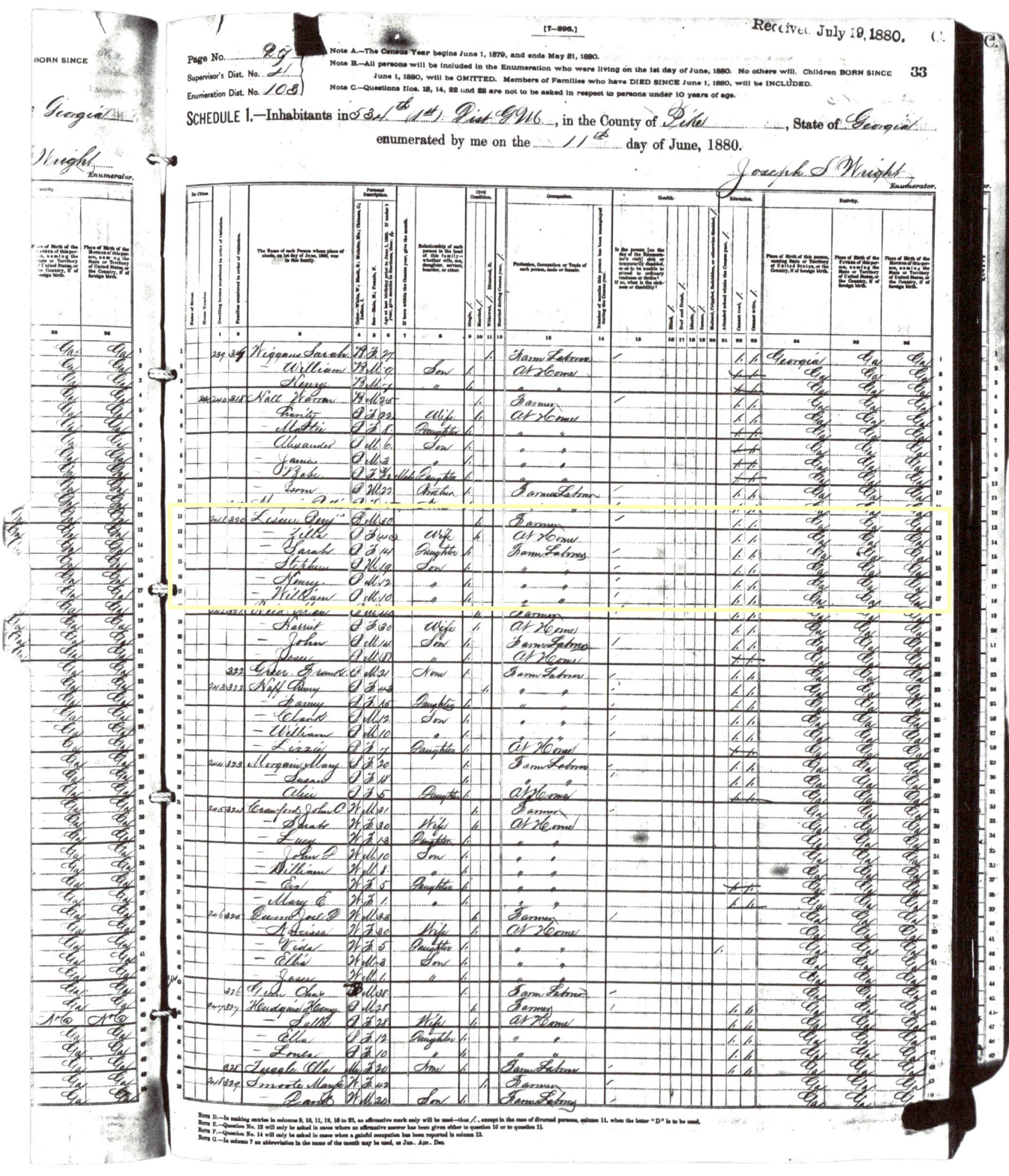

Benjamin, Luscilla, Sarah, Stephen, John Henry and William

Received July 19, 1880.

SCHEDULE 1.—Inhabitants in 534th (1st) Dist G.M., in the County of Pike, State of Georgia, enumerated by me on the 1st day of June, 1880.

Joseph S. Wright, Enumerator

Nancy Lesure (9), Washington (8), Vander (8 mos), Benji (22), Cornelia (26), John (7), William (4)

County of Pike Personal Census | June 16, 1880

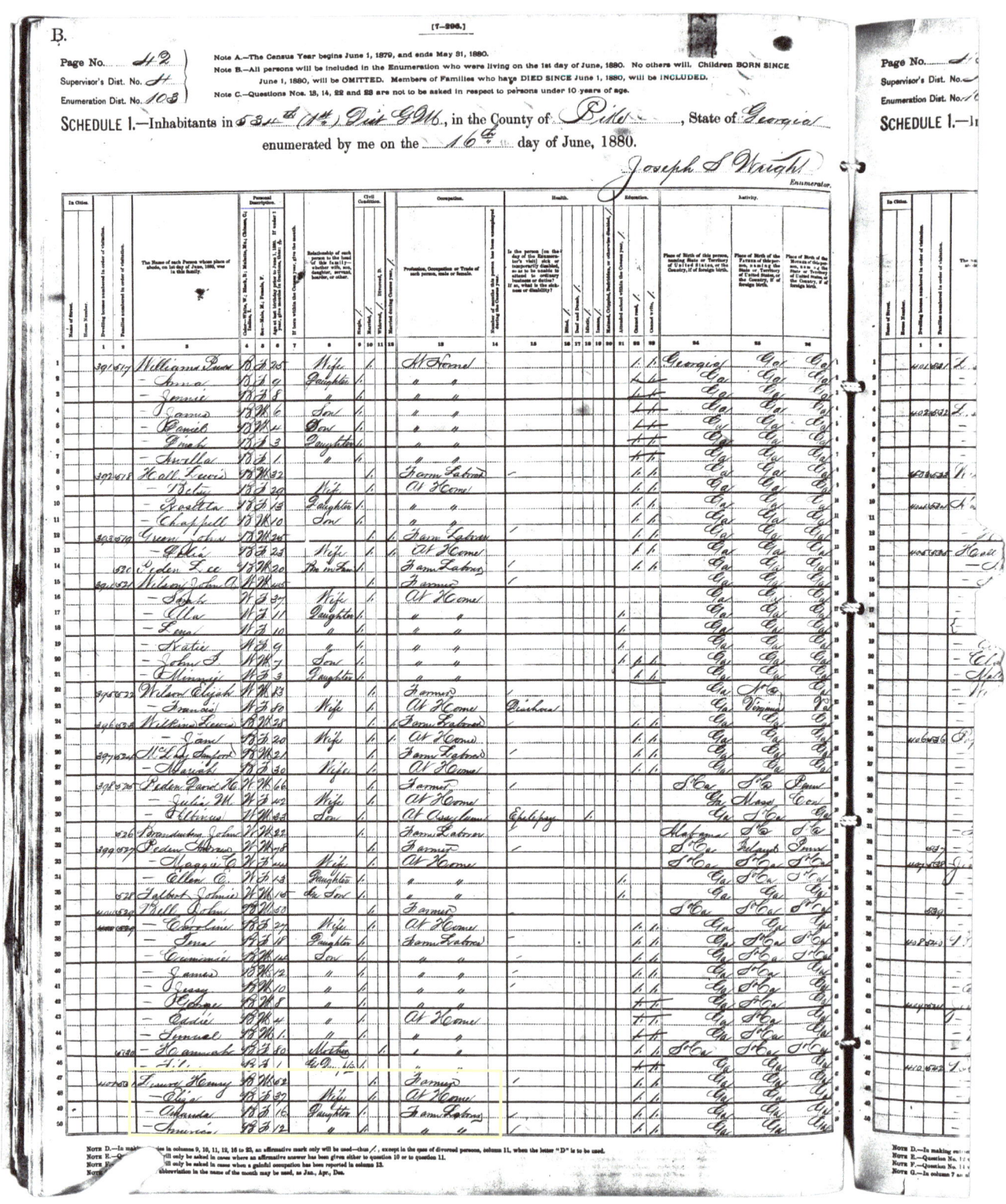

Henry (52), Eliza (37), Amanda (16), America (12)

Relocation to Griffin, Georgia
In the 1880s, Benjamin and his family moved to Griffin, Georgia, where they rented a home on 5th Street. Census data from 1900 describes a household deeply engaged in labor to sustain themselves despite limited opportunities and systemic racial barriers. None of the family members could read or write, but they communicated effectively in English, reflecting the adaptability of the freedmen in navigating their circumstances. Benjamin's children contributed significantly to the household: Stephen worked as a carpenter, Sarah as a floor maid, and Henry, William, and Mattie found employment at a local chair factory.

Economic Challenges and Dependence on Employers
Benjamin's financial situation was intrinsically tied to his employer, T.E. Carson, a former Confederate supporter who wielded considerable influence. Carson's role extended beyond employment, as he was responsible for collecting the $1.00 poll tax that Black citizens were required to pay to be listed to vote. Although, voting rights for slaves and freedmen were not actually rights to vote but simply a way to further ownership and enslavement. This tax was a deliberate measure to disenfranchise freedmen and maintain social and economic subjugation. Additionally, Benjamin's name frequently appeared on Freedman's tax lists, underscoring the enduring impact of slavery-era debts and obligations.

Employers and Connections
Throughout his life, Benjamin worked under various employers, including T.E. Carson, Sullivan Brown, J.W. Sullivan, and Rev. A.G. Pedan. These relationships highlight the limited opportunities available to Black laborers in the South, often marked by economic exploitation and systemic inequities.

T.E. Carson's character further complicates the narrative. A scandal reported in the Jackson Herald on August 22, 1884, revealed that Carson, described as a prominent figure in Pike County, fled with his stepdaughter, abandoning his wife and children. This notoriety provides insight into the power dynamics and moral inconsistencies of the post-Reconstruction elite.

The Death of Benjamin
By 1910, Benjamin had passed away, though the exact date and cause of his death remain unknown. Following his death, "Luscilla," now a widow, lived with her son Henry and his wife Ludie. Demonstrating entrepreneurial prowess, Lucilla operated a laundry service from their home, a business she built making her an entrepreneur.

Scilla's life was defined not by fear but by quiet defiance. Her ability to navigate the constraints of race, her decision to marry for love rather than status, and her determination to survive in a society that sought to define and limit her all speak to the strength of her character. Through her journey, she challenged the rigid racial hierarchies of her time, proving that identity, love, and survival were deeply intertwined in the post-slavery South. Scilla went on to live with her son, John Henry and his family and wives until her death. The exact date of her death is unknown. After her death, Ludie, John Henry's wife, continued to manage the laundry service, ensuring the family's survival, entrepreneurship, and sustaining Benjamin's legacy.

Daniel Lesueur
1853- unknown

Daniel Lesueur was the second-born son of Benjamin and Scilla Lesueur. Born in 1853, he spent most of his adult life in Hollonville, Georgia, as a freedman. During his early years, he was registered as a farmer and, like many other freedmen, was responsible for paying a personal property tax to his many employers, Andrew Wier Blake, also known as "A.W. Blake" being one. As a freedman, Daniel was also registered to vote in the county.

Daniel married Peggy Lesueur (maiden name unknown), a homemaker born in 1858 according to census data. Together, they were recorded in the federal census as parents to eight children, seven of whom were their biological children:

- + Mary Jo Milner (b. 1875)
- Willie (b. 1880)
- Silla (b. 1883)
- Lou E. (b. 1883)
- Fletcher (b. 1885)
- Stephen (b. 1889)
- Charlie (b. 1891)
- Edgar (b. 1892)

Among Daniel's children, Fletcher is traceable throughout history and stands out as a brother to John Henry and one of many uncles of Henry T. He is particularly notable for maintaining close ties with Henry T.'s children and their mother, Ethel Lucier.

Isaac Lesueur
1790 - unknown

Benjamin F. Lesueur
~1833- ~1906
m. Scilla (Beverley)
1836-unknown

Benjamin Jr. (m. Cornelia) 1852
Daniel (m. Peggy) 1853
Fletcher 1860
Sarah 1866
Stephen 1875
William 1870
John Henry 1872
Mattie 1874
+4 other children unknown

Daniel Lucear
m. Peggy
1853

+ Mary Jo Milner 1875
Willie 1880
Silla 1883
Lou E 1883
Fletcher 1885
Stephen 1889
Charlie 1891
Edgar 1892

Fletcher Lucear
m. Bertha Foxworth
1885

Willie Artemus (m. Jeanette Gamble) 1910-2003
Ozella (m. Willie Byrd) 1912-2003
Eddie (m. Mildred Thompson) 1914-1991
Cartrell (m. Ruby Davis) 1916- 1936
Lamar 1932-2022

Federal Census | Hollonville, Georgia | 1900

 Non-Biological Child

Fletcher Lucear
September 1, 1885- April 8, 1955

Fletcher Lucear was born on September 1, 1885, in Concord, Georgia (also a part of Pike County, Georgia), to Daniel LeSueur. He was named after his father's brother, his Uncle Fletcher LeSueur. In his early years, he worked as a farmer.

On October 18, 1905, he married Bertha Foxworth (b. January 1890- d. November 25, 1948) in Griffin, Georgia. By 1920, they were living on Lifsey Springs Road.

Father of 6 and together, they had five children:

- Willie Artemus (1910- 2003) married Jeanette Gamble
- Ozella (1912-2003) married Willie Byrd
- Eddie (1914-1991) married Mildred Thompson
- Cartrell (1916-1936) married Ruby Davis
- Evelyn (1921-1995) mother: Laura Beckham
- Lamar (1932-2022)

Later in the 1950's, Fletcher and his family relocated to Ohio, where they continued building their lives. He was laid to rest at Green Lawn Cemetery in Columbus, Ohio. Today, Fletcher's last name and his surviving family name deviates from the original spelling and shows up throughout history as "Lucear."

Fletcher Lucear

Bertha Foxworth- Lucear

Marriage License of Fletcher Lesueur and Bertha Foxworth
Griffin- Spalding County, Georgia 1905

Federal Census: Fletcher, Bertha, Eddie, Lamar, Ozella | Franklin, Ohio 1940

Uniquely, Fletcher Lucier was required to register for two drafts in his lifetime- first in 1917 for World War I and again in 1942 for World War II. By the time of his second registration, he had relocated from Concord, Georgia to Ohio. Unlike Henry T. and Willie Lucier, he never served in WWI, nor did he serve in WWII like many of his nephews.

Fletcher's WWI Draft Registration

Fletcher's WWII Draft Registration

Ohio Federal Census | 1950

Fletcher Lucear, 64 (widowed), Eddie L. Lucear 35, (never married)

Of Fletcher and Bertha's five children, two left a documented trail that allowed for further research: Willie Artemus and Eddie Lucear. Eddie Lucear, following in the footsteps of his cousins- the children and grandchildren of Henry T.- answered the call to serve in World War II. His dedication and sacrifice did not go unrecognized, as he was honored posthumously for his service, leaving behind a legacy of bravery and commitment to his country.

Willie Artemus Lucear
October 11, 1910- June 13, 1991

Willie Artemus Lucear, the eldest son, was born on October 11, 1910, in Concord, Georgia, to Fletcher and Bertha Lucear. He was one of five children. He passed away at 80 in Columbus, Ohio. He was the father of three children:

- Juanita
- William
- Peggy

Jaunita Lucear

Federal Census | Willie A., Jeanette, Juanita, William D., Peggy M. Franklin, Ohio 1940

Eddie Lucear Sr.
July 22, 1914- August 27, 1991

Eddie Lucear, the third-born child of Fletcher and Bertha, was born on July 22, 1914, in Concord, Georgia. He married Mildred Thompson in 1957 and passed away on August 27, 1991, at the age of 77. Eddie was buried at Jefferson Barracks National Cemetery in St. Louis, Missouri. Historical accounts show that he was the father of five children; 3 sons and 2 daughters.

Eddie Lucear Sr.
WWII Registration and Headstone

Private First Class Eddie Lucear Sr. enlisted on September 4, 1942, at Fort Benjamin Harrison in Indiana and served in World War II until his discharge on January 16, 1946.

Willie Lucear
WWII Registration

Willie Artemus Lucear was also a part of the Selective Service Registration for WWII but was not drafted into the military.

William Lesueur
1870- unknown

William Lesueur (later changed to Lucier), the fifth-born child of Benjamin and Scilla Lesueur, was born in 1870. He spent his early years working in a chair factory and living with his parents and siblings in Griffin, Georgia. Census records consistently list him as "Mulatto," a designation that had been used for other family members for nearly a century.

William first married Stella Lucier, with whom he had two children:
- Andrew Lucier (born 1895)
- Benjamin Lucier (born 1898)

The couple later divorced, and Stella remarried Gibson Barnett.

On January 6, 1906, William married Georgia Freeman (born 1884) in Pike County, Georgia. He was 36 years old, and Georgia was 22. Records indicate they did not have children together.

By 1910, census records show Gibson referring to Benjamin as his "stepson." At this time, Gibson, Stella, and Benjamin had moved from Williamson to Atlanta. Benjamin was 12 years old.

Isaac Lesueur
1790 - unknown

Benjamin F. Lesueur
~1833- ~1906
m. Scilla (Beverley)
1836-unknown

Benjamin Jr. (m. Cornelia) 1852
Daniel (m. Peggy) 1853
Fletcher 1860
Sarah 1866
William (m. Georgia) 1870
John Henry 1872
Mattie 1874
Stephen 1875
+4 other children unknown

William Lucear
m. Georgia Freeman
1870- unknown

Andrew Lucier 1895
Banjamin 1898

Pike County Marriage License | 1906

The exact date and cause of William Lucier's death remain unknown. His wife, Georgia Freeman, passed away on December 19, 1953, and is buried at Fuller Chapel in Zebulon, Pike County.

Georgia Freeman
Born March 10, 1884
Died December 19, 1953

Benjamin "Bennie" Lucier
February 17, 1899- June 7, 1946

Among William and Stella's two children, one left a well-documented trail: Benjamin "Bennie" Lucier, their second-born son. Born on February 17, 1899, in Williamson, Georgia, he later moved to Atlanta with his mother. In 1918, after registering for the mandatory military draft, Bennie was selected to serve in World War I. He was deployed to Brest, France, as a member of the 370th Infantry Regiment, part of the 93rd Infantry Division- the first and only all-Black combat division in the U.S. Army during the war.

The 93rd Infantry Division was unique; unlike most American units, it was assigned to fight under French command due to the U.S. military's segregation policies. The division's soldiers, known for their resilience and bravery, faced intense combat and earned distinguished honors, including the French Croix de Guerre. The 370th Infantry, often called the "Black Devils" by German forces, was one of the most decorated units in the war.

After a year of service, Bennie departed France on February 2, 1919, embarking on a seven-day journey by sea. He arrived back in New York, his original departure city, on February 9, 1919.

By 1940, he had married Odetta (maiden name unknown) and settled in Shelby, Tennessee. He initially worked as a laundryman before transitioning to a hotel helper role at the prestigious Peabody Hotel, continuing his career in hospitality after his military service.

It was later discovered that Bennie was not the only Lucier son to serve in World War I- another brother trained at the same military camp and was deployed to the same country.

Crossing the Atlantic aboard the U.S.S. President Grant
The first units of the 93rd Division sailed from Hoboken on December 12, 1917, followed during February, March and April, 1918, by the remainder of the division from Hoboken and Newport News. The various units landed at Brest and St. Nazaire, France.

WWI Draft Registration Card for Bennie Lucier

Form 1 807 — REGISTRATION CARD — No. 41

1. Name in full: Bennie Lusier — Age, in yrs.: 21
2. Home address: Williamson, Ga
3. Date of birth: Dec 3 1895
4. Are you (1) a natural born citizen, (2) a naturalized citizen, (3) an alien, (4) or have you declared your intention (specify which)? Natural Born Citizen
5. Where were you born? Williamson, Ga, USA
6. If not a citizen, of what country are you a citizen or subject? —
7. What is your present trade, occupation, or office? Porter
8. By whom employed? Southern Railway Co
   Where employed? Williamson, Ga
9. Have you a father, mother, wife, child under 12, or a sister or brother under 12, solely dependent on you for support (specify which)? No
10. Married or single (which)? Single — Race (specify which)? African
11. What military service have you had? Rank: None; branch: none; years: none; Nation or State: none
12. Do you claim exemption from draft (specify grounds)? No

I affirm that I have verified above answers and that they are true.

Bennie Lusier (Signature or mark)

REGISTRAR'S REPORT — 10-3-26-A

1. Tall, medium, or short (specify which)? Medium — Slender, medium, or stout (which)? Medium
2. Color of eyes? Black — Color of hair? Black — Bald? No
3. Has person lost arm, leg, hand, foot, or both eyes, or is he otherwise disabled (specify)? No

I certify that my answers are true, that the person registered has read his own answers, that I have witnessed his signature, and that all of his answers of which I have knowledge are true, except as follows:

Maughn (Signature of registrar)

Precinct: 545
City or County: Pike
State: Ga

JUN 5 1917
(Date of registration)

U.S., Lists of Men Ordered to Report to Local Board for Military Duty, 1917–1918

Form 1029 PMGO.
ORIGINAL.

When completed to be mailed by Military Authorities to the Provost Marshal General, Washington, D. C.

10-3-26   APR 19 64

Local Board for the County of Pike
State of Georgia,
Zebulon, Ga.

SHEET No. 2

Date, April 4, 1918.

The selected men herein described, having been inducted into military service on April 3, 1918 (Date.) have this date been entrained for Camp Gordon (Camp or Station.)

This statement consists of 2 sheets.

1 Order No.	2 Serial No.	3 Name.	4 Call No.	5 Primary Industry.	6 Classification. I	II	III	IV	V	7 Failed to report to Military Authorities.
456	807	Bennie Lucier	—	87	Laborer	A					
464	1602	Molton Roberson	—	87	Farm Lab.	A					
465	1119	Glover Newton	—	87	Farm Lab.	A					
485	58	Claude Davis	—	87	Farm Lab.	A					
491	1320	Johnnie Williams	—	87	Farm Lab.	A					
507	1098	Jack Mangham	—	87	Farm Lab.	A					
~~520~~	~~858~~	~~Lewis Sheffield~~		~~87~~	~~Farm Lab.~~	~~A~~					X
96	1476	General S. Knight	—	87	R. R. Lab.	A					
553	886	R.C.F Butler	—	87	Farm Lab.	A					
561	776	West Bussey	—	87	Farm Lab.	A					

Received
APR 17 1918
P.M.G.O.

245

564

On July 25, 1917, the regiment was mustered into service for World War I. The Headquarters, Headquarters Company, Supply Company, Machine Gun Company, Medical Department Detachment, and Companies A through H originated from Chicago, while Company I came from Springfield (Central Illinois), Company K from Peoria (Northwest-Central Illinois), Company L from Danville (Eastern Illinois), and Company M from Metropolis (Southern Illinois). When the unit was federalized for World War I, it was designated as the 370th. Notably, the African American 8th Infantry fought under French command during this time, remaining the only fully black officer-led American unit since the late 19th century.

As the 370th Infantry, the regiment served honorably alongside the French 34th, 36th, and 59th Infantry Divisions, earning streamers for the battles of Lorraine and Oise-Aisne. They participated in key engagements, including Saint Mihiel in 1918, Argonne Forest, St. Gobain Forest, Bosi de Mortier, Mont des Signes, Oise-Aisne Canal, Laon, Grandlup, Soissons, and the Oise-Aisne and Lorraine offensives. One battalion, commanded by Lieutenant Colonel Otis B. Duncan, pursued the retreating enemy until the Armistice halted their advance.

In recognition of their valor, the members of the 370th received 21 Distinguished Service Crosses, one Distinguished Service Medal, and 68 Croix de Guerre. Lieutenant Colonel Otis B. Duncan, who was awarded a Croix de Guerre, also held the distinction of being the highest-ranking African American officer to serve in combat during World War I.

Due to their fierce combat in the Argonne, the regiment earned the nickname "Black Devils" (German: Schwarze Teufel) from the Germans.

Passenger List | Post of Embarkation: Brest France
February 2, 1918

A. G. O., S. D., A. E. F.
Form No. 3.

PASSENGER LIST

Two copies to Steamship Officers (One in envelope directed to the Adjutant General of the Army); one to be retained, and one to be forwarded to the Central Records Office, A. P. O. 717.

Name of Ship .... Port of Embarkation BREST, FRANCE Date of Sailing .... 191..

NAME	RANK	ORGANIZATION	AUTHORITY	NEAREST RELATIVE		
				Name	Address	Relationship
132 MORGAN, IDA 2650066	PVT. INF.	370TH INFANTRY	TO CAMP UPTON FROM BREST FEB 2 NEW YORK	MRS. REBECCA MORGAN.	R. F. D. NO. 1 BOX 18, MIDVILLE, GEORGIA.	MOTHER
133 MORRIS, RICHARD 2463899	PVT. INF.	"		MRS. ELSIE HEAD	ASHVILLE, NORTH CAROLINA.	FRIEND 271
134 MOORE, WILEY 2654599	PVT. INF.	"		MISS ADEA MOORE	SYCAMORE, GEORGIA.	SISTER
135 MOORE, HOWARD 2656877	PVT. INF.	"		MR. JUNE MOORE	R. F. D. NO. 2 STATHAM, GEORGIA.	FATHER
136 MONROE, HENRY 1403141	PVT. INF.	"		MRS. PEARL E. MONROE.	YOAKUM, TEXAS.	MOTHER
137 MIMS, JOHN 2654456	PVT. INF.	"		MRS. ROSA MIMS.	R. F. D. NO. 4, BOX 35, JEFFERSONVILLE GEORGIA.	MOTHER
138 McINTYRE, ELIJAH 3674318	PVT. INF.	"		MRS. RUTH McINTYRE.	WEST FIELD, NEW JERSEY.	MOTHER
139 MAXWELL, WORTHY T. 1403138	PVT. INF.	"		MRS. MATTIE MAXWELL.	1109 SECOND STREET, ORANGE, NEW JERSEY.	WIFE
140 MATHIS, STURGEN S. 2654400	PVT. INF.	"		MRS. CATHERINE MATHIS.	R. F. D. NO. 2 GIRARD, GEORGIA.	MOTHER
141 MASON, GIBBS 3670577	PVT. INF.	"		MRS. ALICE HARRIS.	717 MAIN STREET, NEW BERN, NORTH CAROLINA.	MOTHER
142 MARTIN, SAMUEL 1403136	PVT. INF.	"		MRS. ELLEN FRAZIER.	GLASGOW, KENTUCKY.	MOTHER
143 MARSHALL, LEVY 2656734	PVT. INF.	"		MRS. KATIE MARSHALL.	UPATCE, GEORGIA.	MOTHER
144 MACK, CHARLIE 2649394	PVT. INF.	"		MR. TONTER MACK.	243 SIXTH STREET, MAGNES BORO, GEORGIA.	FATHER
145 LEWIS, LEVI 2649941	PVT. INF.	"		MRS. AZLOME BANKS.	LINKSTON, GEORGIA.	SISTER
146 LUCIER, BENNIE 2649957	PVT. INF.	"		MRS. STELLA BONNETT.	743 SOUTH ORLEANS, MEMPHIS, TENNESSEE.	MOTHER

AUTHORITY FOR SAILING S.O. 9, 1919 JAN 9, 1919, AMERICAN EMBARKATION CENTER, A. E. F., A. P. O. 762.

Total Officers ....
Total Soldiers ....
Total Casuals ....
TOTAL ....

DECLASSIFIED
Authority NND 785095

Army Statement of Service Card

WWII Draft Registration Card

After Serving for almost a full year in Brest France during WWI, Bennie would be mandated to voluntarily submit to the WWII draft registration at the age of 43.

Certificate of Death | Benjamin "Bennie" Lucier
June 7, 1942

Bennie Lucier passed away from a cerebral hemorrhage resulting from hypertension complications in Shelby, Tennessee, on June 7, 1942. He was 43 years old. He is interred at Memphis National Cemetery, Memphis, Tennessee, USA.

LUCIER

JOHN
HENRY

LUCIER

LUCIER

John Henry

John Henry Lucier

John Henry Lucier was born in 1872 on Hollonville Road in Pike County, Georgia, to Benjamin and Scilla Lucier. He was the father of seven children and was married three times- to Ludie Chunn, Harriett Moore, and Elnora Aft Leslie.

In the late 1880s, he moved with his parents from Pike County to Griffin, Georgia.

As a young man, he worked alongside his siblings, William and Mattie, in a chair factory before transitioning to farming, where he employed his brothers. Later in life, he learned the trade of blacksmithing and worked in a blacksmith shop.

The date and circumstances of his death remain unknown.

Born 1872
Died about 1940- 1950
Buried unknown (believed to be Free Liberty Church, Williamson, Georgia

"Henry"

- ## Ludie Chunn
  Born December 1875
  Death Unknown

- ## Harriett Moore
  Born April 1885
  Died September 22, 1927

- ## Elnora Aft Leslie
  Born July 2, 1880
  Died May 15, 1967

Children:
Willie
Henry T.
Teontia
Donoban
Walter
Marie
Thomas

JOHN HENRY LUCIER

John Henry Lucier 1872

John Henry Lucier's story weaves through a transformative period in American history, marked by the end of slavery, Reconstruction, and the long fight for racial equality. Born in October 1872 in Driver, Georgia, now known as Williamson, he was the son of Benjamin and Scilla Lesueur. John Henry's heritage was diverse: he was described as a mulatto- a term used at the time to denote mixed-race individuals, reflecting one Black parent and one white parent. His father, Benjamin, and grandfather, Isaac, were of Creek Muscogee descent, tying the family to the rich cultural traditions of the Indigenous Southeast.

Growing up in the aftermath of the Civil War, John Henry bore witness to a society in flux. Freedmen like his father were navigating a new and precarious social order where freedom often came with lingering constraints. John Henry, the eldest of his siblings, grew into a man deeply rooted in his family's traditions while striving for stability amid the racial and economic challenges of post-war Georgia.

A Complex Family History
Over his life, John Henry married three women, each union leaving a profound imprint on his life and legacy.

Ludie Chunn: The First Wife

- Born: December 1875
- Death: Unknown
- Marriage: Ludie and John Henry married on July 30, 1892, in Pike County, Georgia. This union marked a new chapter in his young adulthood, as he sought to establish a stable home.
- Children: Together, they had six children: **Willie, Henry, Donoban** (likely Donavan), **Walter, Teontia** and **Marie**. Ludie proved to be a devoted wife and mother, raising their children during a time of financial uncertainty and societal prejudice.
- Family Dynamics: The family's interconnectedness extended beyond Ludie's role as a mother to her biological children. Historical records later reveal that Ludie played a nurturing role in the lives of John Henry's children from his subsequent marriages and so did the other wives to her children. Often throughout the receipts of history, it was found that at times, each of the wives would claim each of the children as resident on federal census reports. In a few instances, the kids appeared to live with both of the first two wives at once. This act of familial solidarity speaks to the resilience and adaptability of the Lucier family during a time when community and cooperation were vital for survival.

Pike County Marriage License

Federal Census, 1900 | Henry (30), Ludie (24), Willie (6), Teontia (3), Donoban (4 mos.), Nannie (9)

The Chunn Family

The Chunn family has a long-established presence in both Spalding and Pike County, with historical records tracing their lineage and activities across multiple generations. Archival documents from the Georgia Department of Archives and History, including the Chunn family papers from 1836 to 1925, provide valuable insights into their social, economic, and familial connections during the 19th and early 20th centuries. These records illustrate the family's evolving role within the region, reflecting broader historical trends of the time.

Ludie was born and raised in Molena, Georgia, nestled in Pike County. The Chunn's lives were deeply intertwined with the rural communities of the area, where family ties and shared histories ran strong.

When Ludie's brother, Willie Chunn (b. 1907- d. 1968) passed away, he was living in a small house at the end of Dunn Road, where it met McCrary Road. The road itself bore the name of Mr. John Dunn, who once owned the sprawling property on its south side. His house stood just across Highway 18, near the intersection that locals easily recognized. Time moved on, and by 1967, the modest home that Willie had once occupied had new inhabitants.

George and Mary King had taken up residence there, along with a few others. Family stories recall that George, by then, had lost his sight entirely. The cause was no mystery- years of drinking moonshine had robbed him of his vision. Whiskey had done its damage. Mary, too, was not well. Family accounts suggest she was often confused and forgetful, her mind burdened by the weight of time and hardship.

Still, life in Pike County carried on. The roads, the houses, and the memories of those who once called them home remained woven into the fabric of the community, reminding all who passed by of the lives that had shaped the land and the stories it held.

(1) Ludie's & Willie Chunn's childhood home in Molena, Georgia (2) L/R - Bobbie J. Dixon, Robert Key, Willie Chunn. Robert Key is pictured wearing a Mastermix Feed cap. Mastermix was a turkey feed brand sold by JB Lawrence in Pike Co.

William "Willie" Lusier
November 9, 1893- October 6, 1918

William is the firstborn son of Ludie Chunn-Lucier and John Henry Lucier. He was born on November 9, 1893, in Rover, Georgia, and later moved with his parents to Driver, Georgia, now known as Williamson, residing on Hollonville & Griffin Road. He and Henry T. were born 2 years apart. His short-lived story is traceable beyond his birth because of his connection to Henry T., especially during his military service during World War I.

By 1910, when William was 16 years old, he was working as a farm laborer. On January 6, 1916, William married Rosa Jones, who was born in 1890. Rosa had previously been married to Jack Jones and had a daughter named Lizzie Jones (b. 1909), who by 11 years old was being raised by her aunt and uncle. Historical records do not indicate that William and Rosa had children together, suggesting that Lizzie, Rosa's daughter from her first marriage, was the child William claimed on his WWI draft registration. Rosa also lived in Hollonville, Georgia. Unfortunately, we have not been able to uncover further details about William's lineage beyond his stepdaughter.

In 1917, he registered for the draft of World War I and was subsequently selected, entering the military on April 3, 1918.

Pike County Marriage License | 1916

Military Index Filing

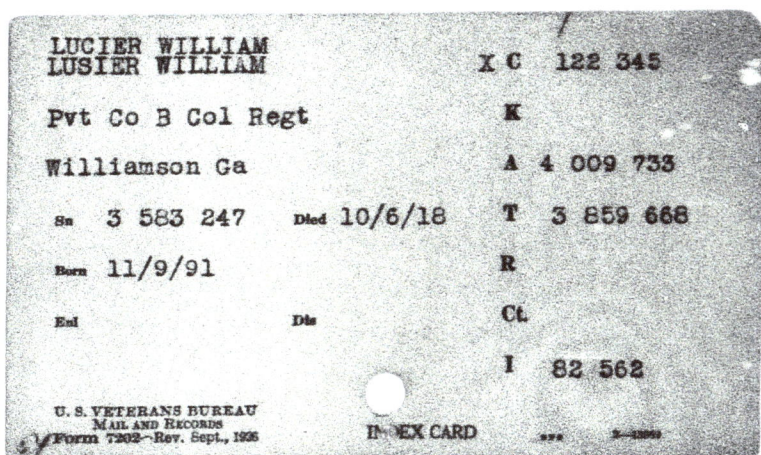

WWI Draft Registration Card for William Lusier

Form 1 813   **REGISTRATION CARD**   No. 75

1. Name in full: **Will Lusier** (Given name) (Family name) — Age, in yrs. **23**
2. Home address: **Williamson Ga** (No.) (Street) (City) (State)
3. Date of birth: **Nov 9 1893** (Month) (Day) (Year)
4. Are you (1) a natural-born citizen, (2) a naturalized citizen, (3) an alien, (4) or have you declared your intention (specify which)?: **Natural Born Citizen**
5. Where were you born?: **Rover Ga USA** (Town) (State) (Nation)
6. If not a citizen, of what country are you a citizen or subject?: —
7. What is your present trade, occupation, or office?: **Farm Laborer**
8. By whom employed?: **A P Dickinson**   Where employed?: **Williamson Ga**
9. Have you a father, mother, wife, child under 12, or a sister or brother under 12, solely dependent on you for support (specify which)?: **Yes Wife and 1 child**
10. Married or single (which)?: **Married**   Race (specify which)?: **African**
11. What military service have you had? Rank: **None**; branch: **None**; years: **None**; Nation or State: **None**
12. Do you claim exemption from draft (specify grounds)?: **Yes — Wife and child dependent**

I affirm that I have verified above answers and that they are true.

Will × Lusier
his mark
(Signature or mark)

10-?

REGISTRAR'S REPORT

1. Tall, medium, or short (specify which)?: **Tall**   Slender, medium, or stout (which)?: **Medium**
2. Color of eyes?: **Dark Brown**   Color of hair?: **Black**   Bald?: **No**
3. Has person lost arm, leg, hand, foot, or both eyes, or is he otherwise disabled (specify)?: **No**

I certify that my answers are true, that the person registered has read his own answers, that I have witnessed his signature, and that all of his answers of which I have knowledge are true, except as follows:

P Vaughn
(Signature of registrar)

Precinct: 545
City or County: **Pike**
State: **Ga**

JUN 5 1917
(Date of registration)

Harriett Moore: The Second Wife

- Born: April 1885
- Died: September 22, 1927
- Marriage: November 8, 1905 John Henry married Harriett Moore. The couple moved to Griffin, Georgia, a growing town with increasing economic opportunities for African Americans. They are believed to have been married for about 5 years or until about 1910.
- Life in Griffin: At their home on 225 N 4th Street, John Henry managed a farm and employed family members, including his brothers, as laborers. This was a bold step toward economic independence during an era when Black landownership and entrepreneurship were fraught with systemic challenges.
- Children: Harriett and John Henry had two children: **An unknown child** and **Thomas**.
- Harriet's Death: Harriett succumbed to carcinoma on September 22, 1927, in Hickory County, Catawba, North Carolina. Her passing marked the end of a pivotal chapter in John Henry's life.

Spalding County Marriage License

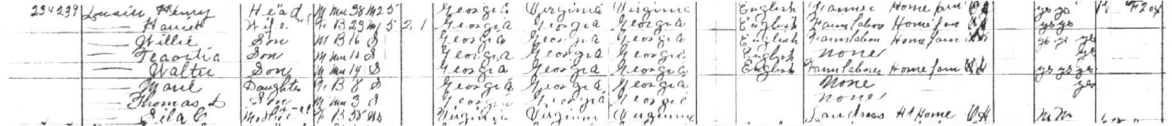

Federal Census, 1910 | Henry (38), Harriett (23), Willie (16), Teontia (10), Walter (14), Marie (8), Thomas (3), Scilla (58)

Griffin, Georgia, City Directory, 1927

Thomas Lee Lusier
September 1, 1906- April 8, 1973

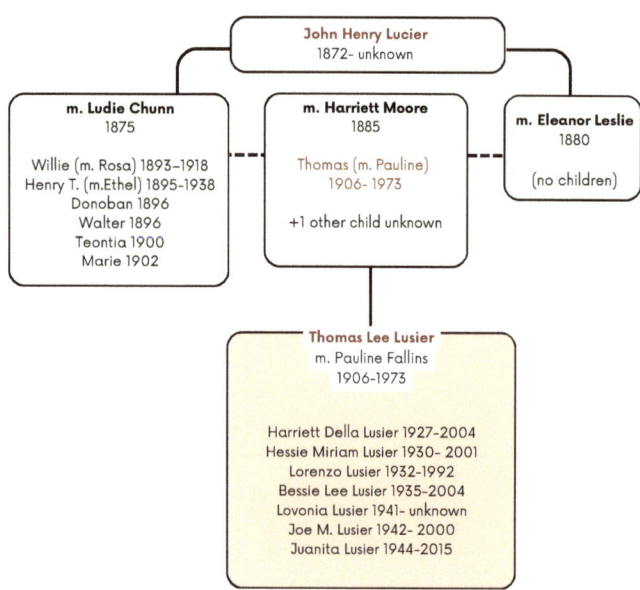

Pauline Fallins- Lusier
(b. 1907- d. 1990)

One of John Henry and Harriett's son, other than Henry T. was Thomas Lee Lusier. He was born August 22, 1906 in Williamson, Georgia. Thomas married Pauline Fallins who was from Roberta, Georgia. Thomas and his family lived in Griffin, Georgia in his early life where he was a driver for a Wholesale Grocer in 1930.

Together, the had 7 children. Their names are Harriett Della Lusier (1927-2004), Hessie Miriam Lusier (1930-2001), Lorenzo Lusier (1932-1992), Bessie Lee Lusier (1935- 2004), Lavonia Lusier (1942- unknown), Joe M. Lusier (1942-2000) and Juanita Lusier (1944-2015).

Many of the cousins were good friends with Hessie, but knew her by her marital name, Hessie Blalock. When in fact, she was born Hessie Lusier. Hessie married Thomas Blalock Sr. and shared 5 children. She died in Portsmouth, Virginia on December 24, 2001.

Hessie's sister, Harriett Della Lusier was named for her grandmother, Harriett. Harriett married Mitchell Magee with whom she shared 5 children. She died on April 21, 2004 due to complications of Sepsis and Acute Hepatitis. Harriett is buried in the Oak Hill Cemetary in Gary, Indiana

Hessie Miriam Lusier- Blalock

Harriett Della Lusier- Magee & Family

Harriett's Death

Harriett Moore Lucier passed away at the age of 44 on September 22, 1927, in Hickory, North Carolina. Following her cancer diagnosis, her parents, Frank Moore and Susan Peoples, brought her back to their home to provide care and support during her final months. Despite their efforts, Harriett ultimately succumbed to hepatic carcinoma, commonly referred to as liver cancer. This form of cancer was often linked to underlying liver disease, particularly cirrhosis, and was typically difficult to treat in the early 20th century due to the limited medical advancements of the time.

A secondary contributing cause of death listed on her death certificate was "aspirations," referring to the inhalation of food, liquid, or other substances into the lungs. Aspiration can lead to respiratory complications, particularly in individuals weakened by severe illness.

Harriett was laid to rest on September 24, 1927, at Southside Cemetery in Hickory, North Carolina. The city, located in Catawba County in the western part of the state, has long been known for its rich history in furniture manufacturing, earning it a place as part of the "Furniture Capital of the World."

Harriett Moore Lucier Death Certificate, 1927

Thomas Lusier's WWII Draft registration card. The alignment of dates and events may validate that at the very least, the eldest children of Henry T- James Henry, William Lucier and Catherine Lucier- knew their Uncle Thomas well before he moved to Detroit.

Thomas died in Detroit, Michigan on June 16, 1973.

Elnora Aft Leslie: The Third Wife

- Born: July 2, 1880
- Died: May 15, 1967
- Background: Elnora was a mulatto woman born in Georgia, widowed before her marriage to John Henry. She managed a boarding house in Griffin, where John Henry lived following Harriet's death. Their shared resilience and mutual respect blossomed into a partnership, and the two married in 1940.
- Occupation: Elnora was a self-employed laundress, a trade she likely inherited from her mother-in-law, Scilla. This entrepreneurial spirit resonated with John Henry's own drive for independence and stability.
- Role in the Family: Though Elnora bore no biological children, she became a beloved stepmother to John Henry's children, particularly as they navigated adulthood. Her presence in their lives reflected the extended family's ability to maintain unity through life's challenges.

Early Life and First Marriage

Elnora Aft Leslie was a mulatto woman born in Georgia. In an era shaped by rigid racial and gender expectations, she carved out a life for herself as a widow and entrepreneur. Elnora married Anthony Leslie, and they built a life together until his death, which left her widowed by 1930. This loss profoundly influenced her future path, prompting her to manage a boarding house in Griffin, Georgia.

The boarding house not only provided her with financial independence but also made her an anchor within the community. It served as a sanctuary for workers, boarders, and transients during a period of significant economic and racial challenges in the South. Elnora also supported herself as a self-employed laundress, a trade that required both physical endurance and resourcefulness, traits she exemplified throughout her life.

Meeting and Marrying John Henry Lucier

By the 1930s, Elnora's path crossed with that of John Henry Lucier, a blacksmith and widower. Born in Driver, Georgia, and of Creek Muscogee heritage, John Henry had already lived a full life of hardship, marked by his efforts to support his family as a farmer and tradesman. After the death of his second wife, Harriet, John Henry became a boarder at Elnora's boarding house. He was no longer a farmer but had taken on the trade of Blacksmith and stated that he was a "widower" in the 1930 federal census as Harriett had died in 1927.

Their shared experiences of loss and independence created a bond that culminated in their marriage in 1940. Following their union, historical documentation, including city directories, confirms that the couple resided together at 509 East Central Avenue in Griffin, Georgia.

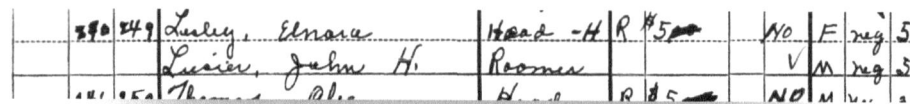

Federal Census, 1930 | Elnora (Head of Household), John Henry (Roomer)

Spalding County Marriage License, 1940

This address, recorded in the 1963 Griffin city phone directory.

Elnora's Role as Stepmother and Caregiver

Although Elnora and John Henry did not have children together, Elnora seamlessly stepped into the role of stepmother to John Henry's children. Family oral histories describe her as a "light-skinned woman with long blonde hair," fueling speculation about her ancestry. Despite family rumors suggesting biological ties, historical records affirm Elnora's identity as a mulatto woman with no biological offspring.

Elnora's bond with her stepchildren and their descendants was deeply significant. She became a maternal figure to the Lucier family, embodying care and stability. Her relationship with Ethel, the wife of Henry T. Lucier (John Henry's son), stands as a testament to the familial loyalty and connections she nurtured. After Henry T.'s untimely death, Ethel took responsibility for ensuring Elnora's well-being in her later years.

Later Years and a Troubling Incident

As Elnora aged, she entered a Brightmore Nursing Home where she spent her final years. However, family accounts reveal a troubling incident during this period. During a visit, Ethel found Elnora in a state of neglect, prompting her immediate removal from the facility. Josie drove and Ethel brought Elnora into her home, ensuring that her final years were spent in comfort and surrounded by family.

Elnora passed away on May 15, 1967, at the age of approximately 84. Despite her long life and significant impact on her family, the exact location of her burial remains unknown. Family records indicate she was interred in Griffin, Georgia, but a fire that destroyed documents from the Negro burial ground has left her final resting place unverified.

Federal Census, 1940 | John Henry (68), Elnora (65)

Legacy and Historical Significance

Elnora's life was a testament to the resilience and adaptability required of African American women during a time of immense social and economic challenges. Her entrepreneurial spirit, as both a boarding house manager and laundress, exemplified the strength and determination needed to navigate a society rife with systemic barriers.

Her role as a stepmother to John Henry's children and her enduring bond with their descendants reflect her unwavering commitment to family and community. The shared life of Elnora and John Henry at 509 East Central Avenue stands as a symbol of their partnership and resilience, tying their stories to the broader history of the LeSueur-Lucier family.

Even in death, Elnora's legacy endures. Though she did not leave biological descendants, her impact as a caregiver, entrepreneur, and beloved figure in the Lucier family remains deeply felt. Her story highlights the complexities of racial identity, the strength of familial bonds, and the enduring spirit of those who persevered through the challenges of their time.

John Henry's Death

Surrounding details and specifics of John Henry's death are still unknown.

Income and Expenditure | Atlanta, Georgia
1900

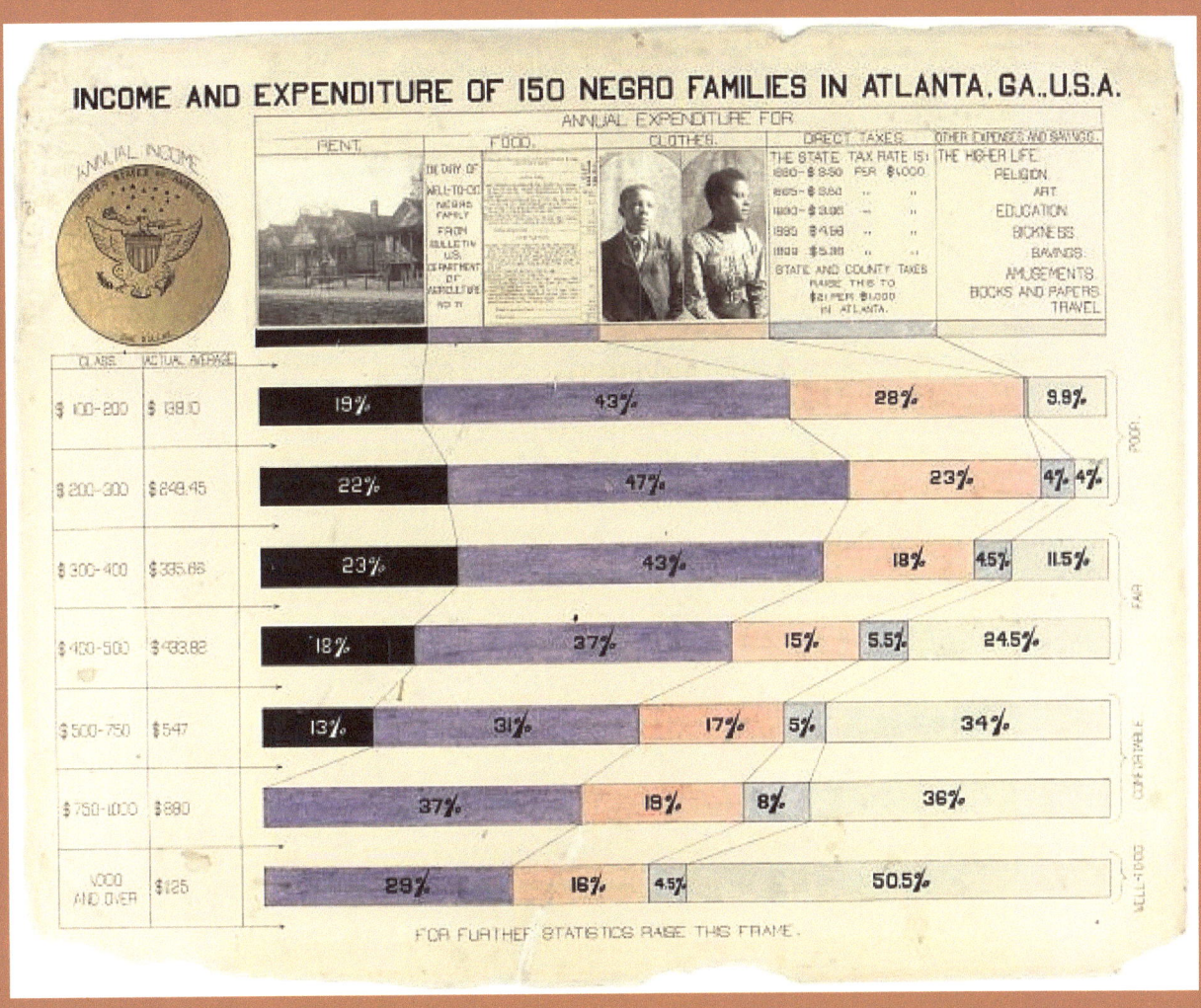

(The Georgia Negro) Income and expenditure of 150 Negro families in Atlanta, Georgia. Bar growth (prepared for the Negro exhibit of the American Section at the Paris exposition Universelle in 1900) shows amount spent on rent, food, clothes, taxes and other expenses by families in various income brackets.

source | Library of Congress

LUCIER

HENRY
& ETHEL

LUCIER

LUCIER

Henry T.

Henry Teasries Lucier

Henry Teasries Lucier, affectionately known as "T," was born in October 1895 to John Henry Lucier and Ludie Churn in Zebulon, Georgia. After serving in World War I from 1918 to 1919, Henry returned home and worked as a section laborer for the Central of Georgia Railway, which operated in Williamson, Georgia.

Henry's life was one of quiet dedication to his family, community, and work. He passed away on October 12, 1938, in Tuskegee, Alabama, at the age of 42. Three days later, he was laid to rest in Williamson, Georgia, at Free Liberty Methodist Church.

Children:
James Henry Lucier
William Lucier
Catherine Lucier
Hermon Lucier
Sarah Lucier
Eleanor Floyd
Ben Lucier
Jeanette Lucier
Josephine Lucier
Josiah Lucier
Harold Lucier

Born November 30, 1895
Died October 12, 1938
Buried Free Liberty Methodist Church, Williamson, Georgia

Buffalo Soldier

Private Henry T. Lucier

**92nd Infantry Division
UNITED STATES ARMY**

Ethel Lindsey

Born May 4, 1901
Died December 2, 1984

WWI Draft Registration Card for Henry T. Lusier

Form 1   808   REGISTRATION CARD   428 | No. 81

1. **Name in full:** Henry Teastrio Lusier   **Age, in yrs:** 21
2. **Home address:** Williamson, Ga
3. **Date of birth:** Nov 30 1895
4. **Are you (1) a natural-born citizen, (2) a naturalized citizen, (3) an alien, (4) or have you declared your intention (specify which)?** Natural Born Citizen
5. **Where were you born?** Zebulon, Ga, USA
6. **If not a citizen, of what country are you a citizen or subject?**
7. **What is your present trade, occupation, or office?** Laborer   30
8. **By whom employed?** H.W. Reynolds
   Where employed? Williamson, Ga
9. **Have you a father, mother, wife, child under 12, or a sister or brother under 12, solely dependent on you for support (specify which)?** No
10. **Married or single (which)?** Single   **Race (specify which)?** African
11. **What military service have you had? Rank:** None; **branch:** None; **years:** None; **Nation or State:** None
12. **Do you claim exemption from draft (specify grounds)?** No

I affirm that I have verified above answers and that they are true.

Henry Teastrio

10-3-26-A
REGISTRAR'S REPORT

1. Tall, medium, or short (specify which)? **Tall** — Slender, medium, or stout (which)? **Medium**
2. Color of eyes? **Dark Brown** Color of hair? **Black** Bald? **No**
3. Has person lost arm, leg, hand, foot, or both eyes, or is he otherwise disabled (specify)? **No**

I certify that my answers are true, that the person registered has read his own answers, that I have witnessed his signature, and that all of his answers of which I have knowledge are true, except as follows:

P. Maughn
(Signature of registrar)

Precinct: JKV
City or County: Pike
State: Ga

JUN 5 1917
(Date of registration)

Georgia's role in World War I (1917-1918) was pivotal, reflecting both its contributions and the challenges it faced during this global conflict. The state hosted more training camps than any other and contributed over 100,000 men and women to the war effort. Alongside its wartime achievements, Georgia endured the devastating influenza pandemic, a tragic maritime disaster, political turmoil, and restrictions on the home front.

War Sentiment in Georgia

When Archduke Franz Ferdinand and his wife were assassinated in Sarajevo, Bosnia, on June 28, 1914, the event that sparked World War I, Georgia's newspapers paid little attention. However, the assassination caused ripples of political instability in Europe, culminating in Germany's attack on Belgium in early August 1914, which ignited war across the continent. U.S. President Woodrow Wilson declared America's neutrality in an August 19, 1914, speech, urging impartiality and fairness.

The war began to affect Georgia indirectly. The torpedoing of the Lusitania on May 7, 1915, caused significant outcry in northern states but elicited muted reactions in Georgia. U.S. Senator Hoke Smith dismissed the need for war, and local newspapers echoed concerns about the economic impact on Georgia's exports, particularly cotton, tobacco, timber, and naval stores, due to the British blockade.

The war also accelerated the Great Migration. African Americans, facing limited opportunities and violence in the South, including lynchings and the rebirth of the Ku Klux Klan, moved north for new war-related jobs. Between 1915 and 1930, Georgia lost more than 10% of its Black population.

The Declaration of War and the Selective Service Act

The U.S. declared war on Germany on April 6, 1917. Despite initial opposition to the war due to economic concerns, Georgia's newspapers quickly shifted to an anti-German, patriotic tone. War fervor swept the state, leading to heightened suspicion of German spies and loyalty tests for labor leaders, teachers, farmers, and immigrants. Farmers were pressured to buy war bonds and drape their plows with American flags, while students and teachers planted "liberty gardens" and avoided German cultural studies.

Baptism for Army Men, Colored troops of the U. S. Army receiving Holy Baptism at the Norcross Rifle Range, Camp Gordon, Ga.

To bolster military forces, President Wilson signed the Selective Draft Act on May 18, 1917. On June 5, eligible men aged 21 to 30 were required to register for the draft. Resistance to conscription was evident in Georgia, with some white landowners preventing Black sharecroppers from registering. U.S. Senator Thomas Hardwick, Rebecca Latimer Felton, and Thomas E. Watson opposed the act. Watson even defended two Black men jailed for failing to register, but the court upheld the act's constitutionality. Over 500,000 men registered in Georgia.

Federal Installations and War Camps
Georgia housed five major federal military installations in 1917, including Fort McPherson near Atlanta and Fort Oglethorpe near the Tennessee border. Fort Screven on Tybee Island defended Savannah's coast, while Augusta hosted both a federal arsenal and Camp Hancock, one of the army's first airfields.

Numerous war-training camps were established. Camp Gordon in Chamblee trained the famous Eighty-second All-American Division, while Augusta's Camp Hancock hosted the Twenty-eighth Keystone Division. Camp Wheeler in Macon trained the Thirty-first Dixie Division, which included over 12,000 Georgians. Specialized camps, such as Camp Greenleaf for medical staff and Souther Field for pilots, prepared troops for specific roles.

Contributions of the Creek Muscogee People
Among the diverse populations contributing to the war effort were members of the Creek Muscogee Nation. The Creek, indigenous to Georgia and surrounding regions, had a complex history of displacement, yet many of their descendants answered the call to serve during World War I.

One notable example was George H. Grayson, a Creek Muscogee man who enlisted in the U.S. Army during the war. Like many indigenous soldiers, he faced challenges of navigating dual identities: preserving his cultural heritage while serving a nation that had historically marginalized his people. Indigenous servicemen often brought unique skills to the battlefield, including exceptional endurance, tracking abilities, and a deep understanding of natural landscapes, which proved valuable in trench warfare and reconnaissance missions.

After the war, Creek veterans played vital roles in their communities, using their military experiences to advocate for indigenous rights and greater recognition of their contributions. Their service is a poignant reminder of the patriotism and sacrifices of Native Americans, even in the face of systemic inequities.

The Otranto Disaster
On September 25, 1918, around 690 soldiers, mostly Georgians from Fort Screven, boarded the British liner Otranto. On October 6, a gale-force storm in the Irish Sea caused the troopship Kashmir to collide with the Otranto, leaving it disabled and drifting toward Scotland's rocky coast. The ship eventually broke apart and sank, killing approximately 370 men, including an estimated 130 Georgians.

County of Pike Military Induction
Camp Gordon Entrainment | April 1918

Form 1029 PMGO.

ORIGINAL.

When completed to be mailed by Military Authorities to the Provost Marshal General, Washington, D. C.

10-3-26 APR 19 64

Local Board for the County of Pike
State of Georgia,
Zebulon, Ga.

Sheet No. 1

Date, April 4, 1918.

The selected men herein described, having been inducted into military service on April 3, 1918 have this date been entrained for Camp Gordon

(Camp or Station.)

This statement consists of 2 sheets.

1 Order No.	2 Serial No.	3 Name	4 Call No.	5 Primary Industry	6 Classification I	II	III	IV	V	7 Failed to report to Military Authorities.
101	757	John Brown	87	Farm Lab.	A					
106	1560	Ben Fletcher	87	Laborer	A					
147	1509	Fred Stanley	87	Farmer	A					
149	525	Charlie Mitchell	87	Farmer	A					
154	66	Edd Dix	87	R.R. Laborer	A					
181	1430	Tom Collier, Jr.	87	Farm Lab.	A					
266	1425	S. T. Thomas	87	Farm Lab.	A					
274	926	Junius Evans	87	Laborer	A					
284	1097	Joe Norman Mabry	87	Farm Lab.	A					
303	1507	Luther Roberts	87	Farm Lab.	A					
334	49	John W. Crittle	87	Farm Lab.	A					
344	1464	Thomas J Hixon	87	Farm Lab.	A					
346	1077	Frank Huguley	87	Farm Lab.	A					
369	492	Will Parker	87	Farm Lab.	A					
370	1201	Charlie Settles	87	Farm Lab.	A					
380	1596	Cottrell Cain	87	Farm Lab.	A					
396	1411	~~Albert Matthews~~	87	Farm Lab.	A					X
400	1393	Hick Fincher	87	Saw Miller	A					
403	970	~~Willie McKinley~~	87	Farm Lab.	A					X
416	935	John H. Hicks	87	Farm Lab.	A					
420	1590	Edd Dallas	87	Farm Lab.	A					
421	113	Roy Colvin	87	Farm Lab.	A					
428	808	Henry T. Lucier	87	Farm Lab.	A					
438	940	Alfred Hicks	87	Farm Lab.	A					
445	989	Lewis A. Pote	87	Farm Lab.	A					
455	133	Jesse Jefferson, Jr.	87	Farm Lab.	A					

Received APR 17 1918 P.M.G.O.

Camp Gordon 1917-1919

3002. INFANTRY DRILL—PORT ARMS.

1918 Commission Roster | "Names, Present and Absent, and Bank"

NAMES, PRESENT AND ABSENT, AND RANK	WHEN ENLISTED	All present and mustered except those indicated in this column by the word (Absent)	REMARKS
85. Kyle, John	Apr 29/18		2650280 Transferred to 27th Lab Bn QMC Camp Wheeler Ga May 22/18 per tel AGO May 15/18
86. Lee, David L.	Apr 3/18		2649254 Transferred to 1st Tr Bn June 2/18 per GO 1 Hq 157th DB June 1/18
87. Lee, Sylvester	Apr 3/18		2649275 Transferred to 1st Tr Bn June 2/18 per GO 1 Hq 157th DB June 1/18
88. Lovett, Buster	Apr 4/18		2649726 Transferred to attached to 9th Co June 1/18 per VOCO 157th DB Sd
89. Lovingood, Patrick	Apr 4/18		2649742 Transferred to 1st Tr BN June 2/18 per GO 1 Hq 157th DB June 1/18
90. Lusler, Bennie	Apr 5/18		2649967 Transferred to attached to 9th Co June 1/18 per VOCO 157th DB Sd
91. Lusler, Henry T.	Apr 3/18		2649203 Transferred to attached to 9th Co June 1/18 per VOCO 157th DB Sd
92. Lynch, Perry	Apr 29/18		2650429 Transferred to attached to 9th Co June 1/18 per VOCO 157th DB Sd
93. McAffee, Matthews	Apr 29/18		2650501 Transferred to 27th Lab Bn QMC Camp Wheeler Ga May 22/18 per tel AGO May 15/18
94. McWilliams, Albert	Apr 29/18		2650579 Transferred to 27th Lab Bn QMC Camp Wheeler Ga May 22/18 per tel AGO May 15/18
95. McCauley, Elester	Apr 4/18		2649274 Transferred to 1st Tr Bn June 2/18 per GO 1 Hq 157th DB June 1/18
96. McCrary, Jim	Apr 4/18		2649248 Transferred to 1st Tr Bn June 2/18 per GO 1 Hq 157th DB June 1/18
97. McCrary, J. F.	Apr 4/18		2649880 Transferred to 1st Dev Bn June 2/18 per GO 1 Hq 157th DB June 1/18
98. McLaughlin, Joseph	Apr 4/18		2649908 Transferred to attached to 9th Co June 1/18 per VOCO 157th DB Sd

Report of Co "E", Development Battalion, No. 2. Camp Upton, N.Y. at Midnight September 30th, 1918

Report of Co "E", Development Battalion, No. 2, Camp Upton, N.Y.
At midnight Sept. 30th, 1918.

SHEET No. 7

Privates (continued)

#	Name	Number
377	Wallace, Vernon	3722262
378	Wallace, Will	2046309
379	Walters, Herbert	4155464
	Joined 21st.	
380	Ward, Willie	2561371
381	Watkins, Colonel	3723185
382	Watley, Ben	3203849
	Joined 21st.	
383	Watson, Edward	3723179
384	Watson, Sam	1694623
385	Webster, William M.	4151825
	Joined 1st.	
386	West, James L.	4150284
387	Weston, James	3725428
388	Whitaker, Jim	2089498
389	White, Edgar	4151189
	Joined 1st.	
390	White, John	3199301
391	Whitfield, Paul C.	4150515
392	Whitson, John	2073750
393	Wilkerson, Jesse	1729371
394	Williams, Frank W.	4150190
	Joined 3rd.	
395	Williams, John H.	2089505
396	Williams, Jesse	4151194
	Joined 1st.	
397	Williams, Oscar	4153029
	Joined 19th.	
398	Willis, Lawrence	3725599
399	Wilson, Daniel L.	2076850
	Joined 1st.	
400	Wilson, Ernest	2562626
	Joined 21st.	
401	Winston, James A.	2073712
402	Winston, Lee A.	1729523
	Joined 19th.	
403	Wise, Dave	463768
	Joined 19th.	
404	Wood, Hezekiah	2167167
405	Woolridge, Andrew	4151455
	Joined 21st.	
406	Worrol, Arthur	4149077
407	Wright, Thomas	4152673
408	Wyke, William H.	3203255
	Joined 21st.	
409	Young, Frank	2562317
410	Young, Enoch	4149547
411	Pugh, Isaac	3726333
	Joined 21st.	
412	Ross, Shephard	3723797
	Joined 14th.	

ATTACHED FOR DUTY.

Privates.

#	Name	Number
1	Brown, William	3724054
	Awol since 8/29.	
2	Butler, John	3724886
	Awol since 8/29	
3	Council, John	2818528
	Joined 27th.	
4	Dilbert, Chester	3726963
5	Enoch, Anthony	1688331
	Joined 27th.	
6	Grant, John J.	4155464
	Joined 12th.	
7	Griffin, William	2204702
8	Hall, Fate	2717628
	Joined 27th.	
9	James, Pete	2243135
10	Jones, Horace	1729321
11	Lucier, Henry T.	2646283
	Joined 27th.	
12	Penha, Ludwig	3203631
	Awol since 8/29	
13	Raymond, Monroe	2561342
14	Taylor, Joel	2466475
15	Waddell, Frank	3203819
	Awol since 8/29	
16	Washington, George S.	3199888
17	Wiggins, Dorsay	3202953
18	Williams, Benny	2882601

Henry Teasries Lucier

Henry Teasries Lucier, a 22-year-old African American from Georgia, was drafted on April 3, 1918, into the 152nd Depot Brigade at Fort Gordon. He later served in the 92nd Infantry Division, a segregated unit nicknamed the "Buffalo Soldiers." The "Buffalo Soldiers" nickname was originally given to African American cavalry regiments by Native Americans in the 19th century. It is believed the name referred to their fierce fighting spirit and the texture of their hair, which resembled the coat of a buffalo. This division, along with the 93rd Infantry Division, represented the only Black combat units in World War I. Although 380,000 African Americans served in the military, including 200,000 sent to Europe, segregation limited their roles. More than half were assigned to labor battalions, building roads, bridges, and trenches. Only 42,000 saw combat. Henry T. was sent by ship to fight in Ainvelle, Vosges, France.

Henry's brother mentioned earlier, Will Lucier, also enlisted and sent from Williamson to Camp Wheeler in Macon, Georgia, but succumbed to pneumonia in France on October 6, 1918- two months after enlisting. His body never made it back home. Henry T. survived and returned home, discharged on January 17, 1919. The experiences of African American soldiers abroad, particularly under the less segregated French military, fueled demands for civil rights upon their return. These veterans became catalysts for the civil rights movement, challenging racial inequality in a nation they had fought to defend. He was 24 years old at the time of his death.

1918 | Will Lucier's Military Death Record

The 92nd Infantry Division, known as the Buffalo Soldiers Division, played a pivotal role in World War I during its deployment to France in 1918. Composed primarily of African American soldiers under the leadership of white officers, the division arrived in Europe in the summer of 1918 as part of the American Expeditionary Forces led by General John J. Pershing.

The division was assigned to the western front, where it fought in the Meuse-Argonne Offensive, one of the largest and most decisive battles of the war. This offensive, launched in September 1918, was a crucial effort by Allied forces to break through German lines and force an end to the conflict. The 92nd Infantry Division's units operated in the Argonne Forest region, enduring harsh combat conditions and navigating the complexities of trench warfare.

92nd Infantry Division | Ainvelle, Vosges, France
1917–1919

Insignia shoulder patch for the 92nd Infantry Division

Helmet worn by Peter L. Robinson, Sr. during World War I

Reproduction patch with Red Hand emblem

Uncle Sam Provides for Comfort of His Soldiers. Colored Troops En Route to France Taking Train Rest at Railway Division Point

109

368 Inf, 92nd Div advancing on camouflaged road - Binarville (Argonne) Oct. 1, 1918

Watching "Hun" Planes - 317th Supply Train - Belleville, Oct. 1918

3d Bn. 366 Inf. 92nd Div. at Gas Mask Drill - Ainvelle, Vosges, France - Aug 8, 1918.

366 Inf. 92nd Div. Ainville, Vosges, France - Aug 11, 1918

367 Machine Gun Bn. enroute to Argonne Front passing thru St. Minehould
Sept. 16, 1923

Graves of 92nd Div - Pont du Mosson, Meurthe et Moselle, Nov. 24, 1918

25942
Truck Train unloading 366 Inf. Bruyens, Vosges, France. Aug 12, 1918

39650
Mess 317 Supply Train - Belleville Meuse, Oct 12, 1918

Q. M. Hdqrs. 92nd Div. - Bourbaine les Bain, Hte. Marne, France Aug 11, 1918

German Alsacians captured by 42nd Div - St Die, Vosges Sept 14, 1918

Blacksmith Shop, 366 Inf, Sergieux, Hte. Marne, France, Aug 1, 1918.

325 Field Signal Bn. 42nd Div. Stringing Lines - Binarville (Argonne) Oct 1, 1918.

"A Close Shave" - 311th Supply Train, Belleville, Meuse
Oct. 12, 1918

Regimental Hdqrs. - Doorbeun les Dune - Oct. 2, 1918

367 Inf 92nd Div. On way to Marbache Mthe et Moselle, Oct. 12, 1918

Mess - M.T.R.S men 92nd Div. Belleville, France Nov. 17, 1918

panoramic photograph of M Company, 365th Infantry, 183d Brigade

panoramic photograph of Camp Grant officers

panoramic photograph of 183d Brigade of the 92d Infantry Division

Despite systemic racism and the challenges of segregation within the military, many soldiers of the 92nd Division displayed exceptional courage and determination. They faced skepticism from some within the U.S. Army about their abilities, but their performance on the battlefield helped challenge these prejudices. Their contributions underscored their commitment to the war effort and demonstrated their capability under fire.

The experiences of the 92nd Infantry Division during World War I hold historical significance, not only for their contributions to the Allied victory but also for highlighting the racial inequities within the U.S. military. The division's service marked an important chapter in the ongoing struggle for recognition and equality for African American soldiers.

92nd infantry "Buffaloe Soldiers" Division

Headquarters Port of Embarkation, Hoboken, New Jersey | Passenger List of Organizations and Casuals

Military Index Filing

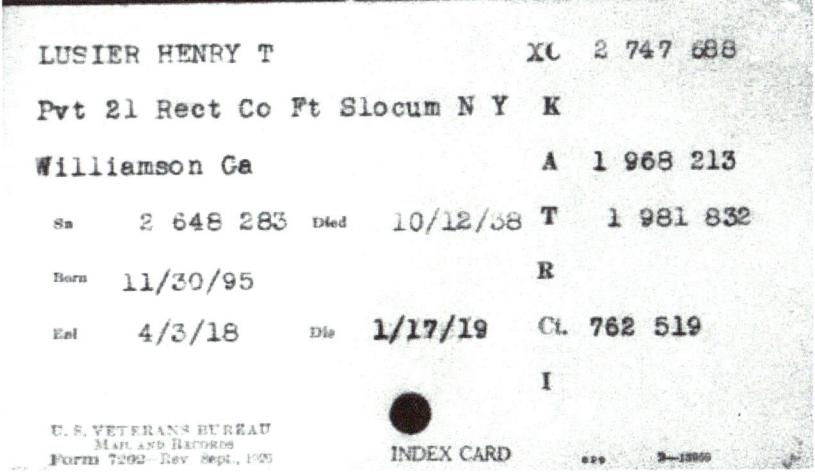

The Influenza Pandemic
In late September 1918, new draftees at Fort Screven reported severe illness, marking the arrival of the Spanish flu. By October 1, cases at Augusta's Camp Hancock surged from 2 to 716 in hours. Camp Gordon soon reported 138 cases. Despite quarantines, the virus spread rapidly, causing significant fatalities among soldiers and civilians. Georgia, however, experienced fewer casualties than other East Coast states.

Remembering the War
World War I officially ended with the Treaty of Versailles in 1919, but hostilities ceased on November 11, 1918, with an armistice. In the aftermath, Americans commemorated the war through Armistice Day, established as a national holiday in 1938 and renamed Veterans Day in 1954. Georgia played a central role in these efforts. Moina Belle Michael, an administrator at the University of Georgia, designed paper poppies to fund wounded soldiers' rehabilitation, inspiring a global tradition of poppy sales for remembrance.

January 17, 1919
Henry was honorably discharged from The United States Army and returned home to Williamson, Georgia.

Military Personnel Card

Williamson, Georgia Train Depot

After his return from the war, Henry started working for the Central of Georgia Railway in the late of 1920. Williamson, Georgia had it's own depot.

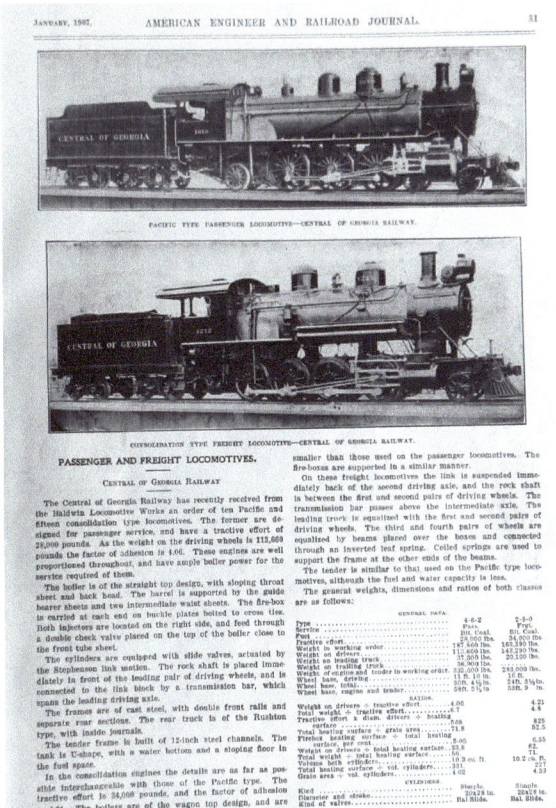

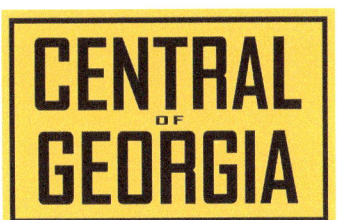

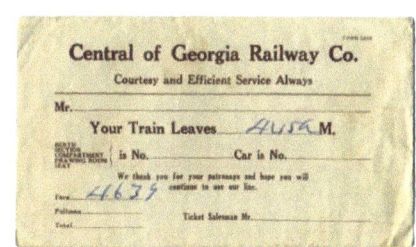

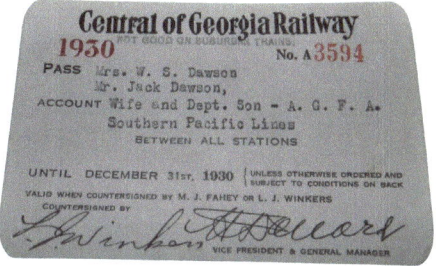

Early Railroad Years, 1830s to the Civil War

Charleston, South Carolina, provided the impetus for rail development in Georgia. In 1830 it began building a 136-mile railroad to Hamburg, on the Savannah River opposite Augusta. Savannah businessmen, worried that Charleston would benefit at their expense, responded by organizing the Central Rail Road and Canal Company. The state legislature, meeting in Milledgeville, issued a charter for the company in December 1833. The canal division of the company was soon dropped in favor of the construction of railroads, which were not as limited as canals with regard to where they could be built. Construction began in December 1835. The Central Rail Road of Georgia eventually became the Central of Georgia Railway, a 190-mile line across the Coastal Plain to Macon.

Meanwhile, construction on the Georgia Railroad between Augusta and Athens and on the Monroe Railroad (later the Macon and Western) between Macon and Forsyth, was in progress. The Georgia Railroad Company was chartered to a group of Athens businessmen in 1833 for the purpose of building a railroad from Augusta west into the interior of the state. In 1835 the charter was amended to allow banking operations, and the name was changed to Georgia Railroad and Banking Company. Company headquarters moved from Athens to Augusta in 1840. The Georgia Railroad was completed to Marthasville (later Atlanta) in 1845.

This abandoned railway line was originally chartered as the Atlanta and Hawkinsville Railroad in 1886. Despite the A&H's intent to build from Atlanta south to Cordele, GA, the line only went as far as Fort Valley by 1888. The line ran parallel to both the Central of Georgia mainline and the Southern Railway mainline between Atlanta and Macon.

During its early years, several passenger trains were run along the line, as evidenced by the 11 passenger stations found along the route, including one in both Atlanta and Fort Valley. The line was renamed to the Atlanta and Florida Railroad before ultimately coming under the control of the Southern in 1895.

The Great Depression in the 1930s resulted in the loss of many lines and the Southern made the decision to redirect traffic from this line to their mainline between Atlanta and McDonough, then to Williamson, where an existing connection with this line was utilized in order to give access along the remainder of this line south to Fort Valley. Despite the new traffic pattern, a 1932 timetable shows at least 6 trains running along the line before the abandonment of the northern portion of the line in 1938.

The southern portion between Williamson and Fort Valley saw continued use for local traffic by the Southern up until the mid-1970s, when the northern end of the line between Williamson and Roberta was pulled up in 1977.

Today, the segment between Roberta and Fort Valley still sees service, as a local shortline operator serves a sand mine in that area.

1930 Henry T. Lucier and two white males standing in front of the Central of Georgia Railroad Train

Ethel

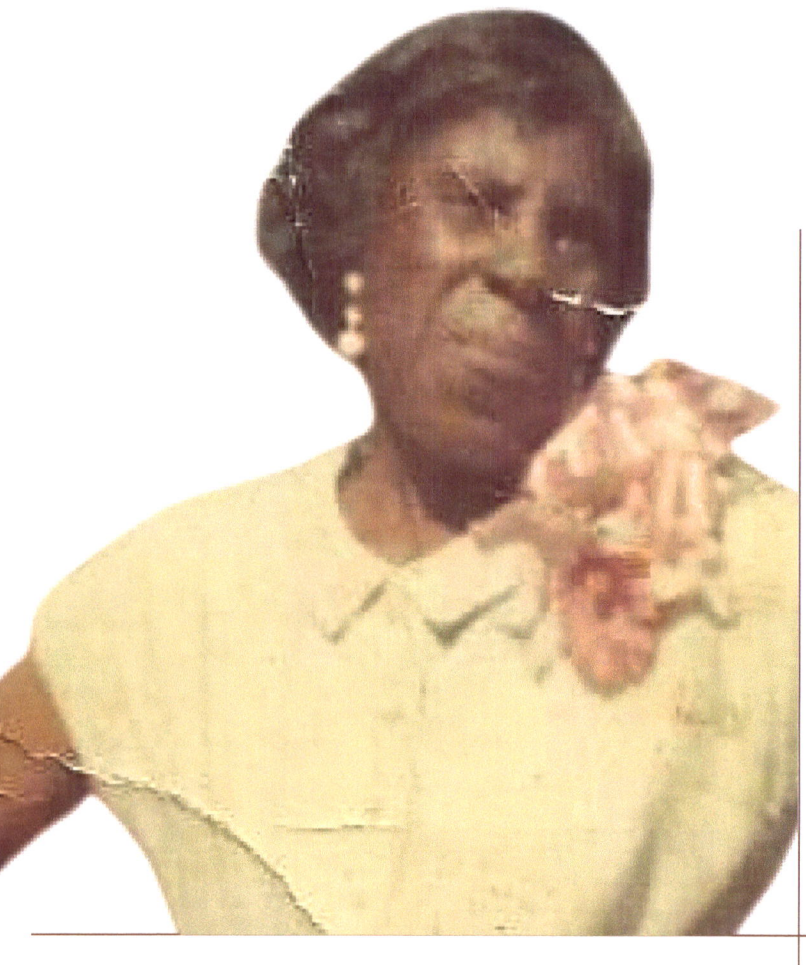

Ethel V. Lindsey Lucier

Ethel V. Lindsey was born on May 15, 1901, at the turn of the century, to James E. Lindsey and Cora Reeves in Driver, Georgia, a small rural community that is now known as Williamson, Georgia, located in Pike County. She was the eldest of eight children, setting the tone as a caregiver and leader for her younger siblings:

- Estella Lindsey 1905
- Willie Bell Lindsey 1906
- Inez Lindsey 1907
- WT Lindsey 1908
- Robert Lindsey 1909
- Julia Lindsey 1912
- James Lindsey 1913
- Ben Lindsey 1919
- Ermatine Lindsey 1921

Born May 4, 1901
Died December 2, 1984
Buried Free Liberty UMC Church, Williamson, GA

Mama

Children:
James Henry Lucier
William Lucier
Catherine Lucier
Hermon Lucier
Sarah Lucier
Ben Lucier
Jeanette Lucier
Josephine Lucier
Josiah Lucier
Harold Lucier
+ Azzie Marshall

Henry Teasries Lucier

Born November 30, 1895
Died October 12, 1938

Henry T. and Ethel's Marriage License, December 17, 1920, Pike County Georgia

On December 17, 1920, Henry T. Lucier married Ethel Lindsey in Pike County, Georgia.

Ethel Lindsey

Williamson and Pike County in the Early 20th Century
In the early 1900s, Pike County, Georgia, was deeply entrenched in the agrarian economy of the South, shaped by its history of slavery and Reconstruction. Black residents, who made up a significant portion of the population, were predominantly sharecroppers, tenant farmers, or laborers working on white-owned farms. Williamson, like many small towns in the region, was built around agriculture, with crops such as cotton, tobacco, and corn dominating the local economy.

The social climate of the time was defined by the oppressive structures of Jim Crow laws. Racial segregation permeated every aspect of life, from schools and churches to transportation and public facilities. Black residents faced systemic discrimination, economic hardships, and the constant threat of racial violence, with the Ku Klux Klan maintaining a strong presence in the region. For Black women like Ethel, survival required immense resilience and adaptability.

Marriage and Family Life
At 19, Ethel married Henry T. Lucier on December 17, 1920, in Pike County. The couple began their life together in a world where marriage and family were central to survival. By 1921, they welcomed their first child, James Henry Lucier, and over the next 18 years, Ethel gave birth to nine more children: **William, Catherine, Hermon, Sarah, Ben, Jeanette, Josephine, Josiah,** and **Harold**.

While raising her children, Ethel contributed to the family's income by working as a farmhand. She labored in the fields, picking cotton, peaches, and harvesting crops Though this level of work was a grueling and poorly paid job that was essential for the survival of many Black families, Ethel refused to clean after white people and preferred field work over domesticated labor. This was a common reality for women in Williamson, where community life revolved around the rhythms of planting and harvesting seasons.

United States Census | Pike County, Georgia | April 5, 1940

Henry T's Death

Henry T. sought treatment at the Veterans Hospital for Crohn's disease. Henry started having issues with digestion. It is said that he was unable to keep foods from being regurgitated. He was facing a challenging battle with Crohn's disease, a condition poorly understood in his time. In 1938 Georgia, a Black man suffering from Crohn's disease would face immense hardship. Medical understanding of the condition was limited, and treatment options were scarce, especially for Black individuals due to systemic racism and segregation. Access to healthcare was severely restricted, with few hospitals willing to treat Black patients, and those that did were often underfunded and poorly equipped. Pain, malnutrition, and debilitating symptoms like abdominal pain, diarrhea, and weight loss would likely go untreated. Social stigma and lack of awareness about the disease would compound his suffering, leaving him with little support or relief. His experience would be marked by neglect, discrimination, and the harsh realities of living with a chronic illness in a deeply segregated and unequal society. Surgery, a common option today, was rarely considered in the 1930s unless life-threatening complications arose.

In the early 1920s, the nearby Tuskegee Institute- a historically Black university- donated land to the federal government to build what was originally dedicated in 1923 as the "Veterans Hospital for Negro Disabled Soldiers." A first of its kind during this era, the VA Hospital admitted Henry T. for diagnosis and treatment.

The "Veterans Hospital for Negro Disabled Soldiers" in 1938

On October 12, 1938, Henry Teasries Lucier took his final breath in Tuskegee, Alabama at the Veterans Hospital for Negro Disabled Soldiers. He was 43 years old. He left behind 10 children ranging from 17 years old to 1 year old, and a 37-year-old and pregnant wife.

October 12, 1938

On the day Henry T. Lucier died, of all places in the world, Tuskegee, Alabama would host a general call for all former enlisted negro servicemen interested in training under an unfunded military program.

A pivotal moment in history unfolded with the establishment of the foundation for the Tuskegee pilot training program. This initiative, driven by the demand for African American participation in aviation and military service, laid the groundwork for the future development of the first Black military aviators in U.S. history. The Civilian Pilot Training Program (CPTP) at Tuskegee Institute (now Tuskegee University) in Alabama was a national aviation training program that trained the first Black USAAF combat pilots: The federal government's Civil Aeronautics Authority (CAA) funded the CPTP in 1939 to provide introductory aviation training to college students. The program was a success, training 435,165 pilots between 1939 and 1944. The CPTP graduated around 2,000 black pilots overall. The program meant individuals previously excluded from pilot training could learn to fly through educational institutions. Suddenly, African Americans and women could pilot planes.

The Tuskegee program, initiated at the Tuskegee Institute in Alabama, was part of President Franklin D. Roosevelt's response to advocacy efforts for racial equality in the armed forces. Though the program officially expanded in subsequent years, the seeds were planted in 1938 when discussions and preliminary steps began to make aviation training accessible to African Americans. His insistence on the segregated training of black pilots was ridiculed by the N.A.A.C.P (National Association for the Advancement of Colored People).

The program not only trained skilled pilots but also broke racial barriers in the military, proving the capabilities of African Americans in roles traditionally denied to them. The Tuskegee Civilian Pilot Training program continued through 1943, at the end of World War II. It trained over 900 black pilots.

Today, we know those pilots as the Tuskegee Airmen.

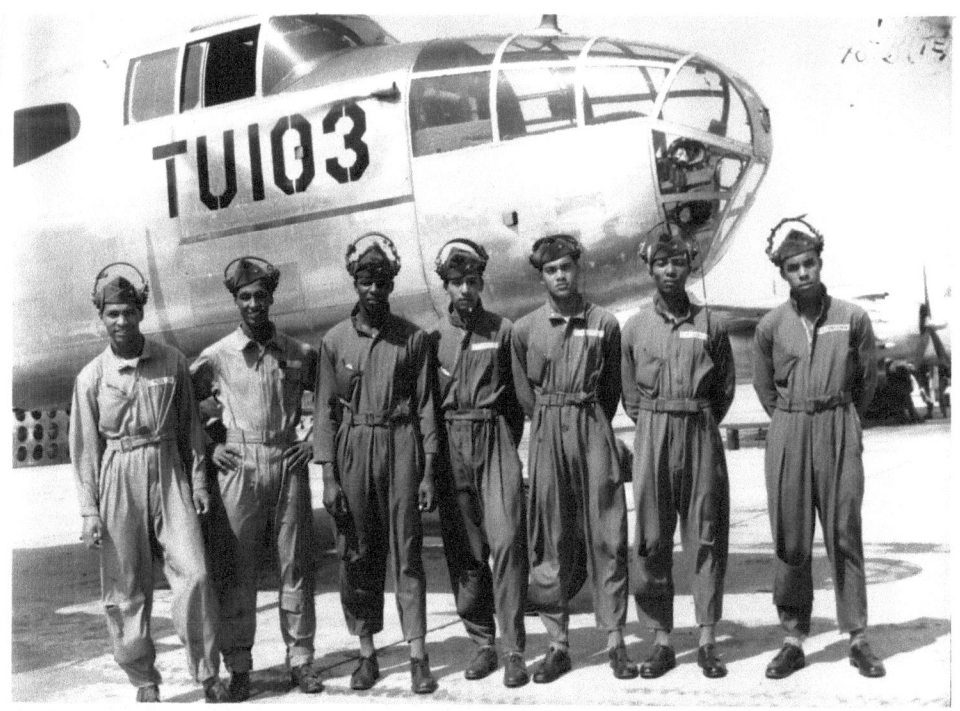

Tuskegee Airmen, 1938

Life After Henry T.
At the time of Henry's death left Ethel a widow at 37, pregnant with their youngest child, Harold, and with nine children to care for.

During this period, the challenges for Black widows in rural Georgia were immense. The economic system of sharecropping often kept Black families in cycles of debt and poverty, and there was little to no social safety net. White landowners controlled much of the local economy, and Black residents who attempted to assert independence often faced violent retribution.

Despite these challenges, Ethel worked tirelessly to keep her family together. Her eldest sons, James Henry and William, soon entered the Army to support the family, while Catherine helped as a housekeeper. Hermon stayed home to assist Ethel with the younger children and work for the railroad.

The Social and Cultural Landscape of Williamson
Williamson was a small, tightly knit community where social dynamics were often influenced by economic disparities and racial tensions. The Black community in Williamson, while marginalized, created its own spaces of support and recreation. There was a street known as "On the Line," lined with modest homes, many of which were formerly slave quarters. This area became a hub for social gatherings and recreational activities for the Black community. To get there from "Dark Town," you would have to walk at night, through the woods with an oil lamp for fear of being rounded up by the Klan.

However, navigating life in Williamson was fraught with danger. Black residents faced significant risks if they were caught traveling at night or found in certain areas deemed "off-limits" by the white population. Stories of lynchings and racially motivated violence were common, creating a constant undercurrent of fear.

Ethel's recreation with friends in these areas provided moments of relief, but these outings also underscored the risks she faced as a Black woman navigating a racially hostile environment.

Resilience and Redemption
After Henry's death, Ethel struggled with alcohol as she coped with her grief. Despite this, she remained deeply committed to her children, eventually overcoming her struggles to rebuild relationships with her family. By the 1950s, Ethel worked as a housekeeper, continuing to provide for her children.

Her sacrifice was further demonstrated in her care for Henry's stepmother, Elnora. Upon discovering that Elnora was being mistreated in a care facility, Ethel took her into her home, ensuring she lived her final years in dignity.

Legacy of Strength
Ethel Lindsey's life was a testament to the strength required of Black women in the rural South. She endured and overcame profound challenges: systemic racism, the loss of her husband, raising ten children as a widow, poverty, and the constant threats of the Jim Crow era. She lived through the Great Depression, the Civil Rights Movement, and profound societal changes that reshaped the South.

Ethel passed away on December 2, 1984, at the age of 83 in Williamson, Georgia. She is buried at Free Liberty United Methodist Church. Her legacy lives on through her descendants, who carry forward the strength and perseverance she embodied. These qualities have become the ethos of the family.

Ethel Lindsey's story is not only one of personal survival but also a reflection of the broader struggles and triumphs of Black families in the rural South during one of the most challenging periods in American history. She lived to be a testament to the survival of the time and existence of her children.

LUCIER

THE CHILDREN

LUCIER

LUCIER

LUCIER

1st Born

James Henry Lucier

Staff Sergeant James Henry Lucier was born on October 13, 1921, in Williamson, Pike County, Georgia, as the first child and son of Henry and Ethel Lucier. James was just 17 years old when his father passed away and 64 at the time of his mother's death. He enlisted in the U.S. Army Corps of Engineers at Fort McPherson on March 28, 1941, and served for 20 years, completing his military service on March 31, 1961. During his distinguished career, James served in both World War II and the Korean War. He achieved the rank of Staff Sergeant (E-6), a role that included leading a squad of 9-10 soldiers and overseeing critical engineering operations. After his return home, James took a job with the Griffin Daily News and held a paper route to fill his day with activity.

James had no biological children however, he adopted and was a devoted father to his only child, Darlene Lucier, and was married once, to Ozzie Anderson. He passed away due to complications of diabetes on November 1, 1989, at the age of 68.

Born October 13, 1921
Died November 1, 1989
Buried Free Liberty UMC, Williamson, Georgia

Ozie Belle Anderson

Birth July 31, 1922
Death July 17, 1980

African-American Engineer Troops

Staff Sergeant James Henry Lucier

UNITES STATES ARMY

For many family members, James was the first individual they had ever witnessed leaving their hometown, boarding a plane, and traveling overseas. He inspired numerous people to pursue similar paths and offered support to many throughout their journeys. Notably, his military service motivated his great-nephew, Karl Wimbush, to enlist in the Marines, and his grandson, Troyius Brown, also dedicated four years to the US Marine Corps. They were not the only ones influenced by his example; many of the family's young men chose to enter military service with James as their inspiration. He was cherished by many, and his daughter, nieces, and nephews hold dear the memories of a kind, generous, and loving man in James.

Children:
+ Darlene Lucier

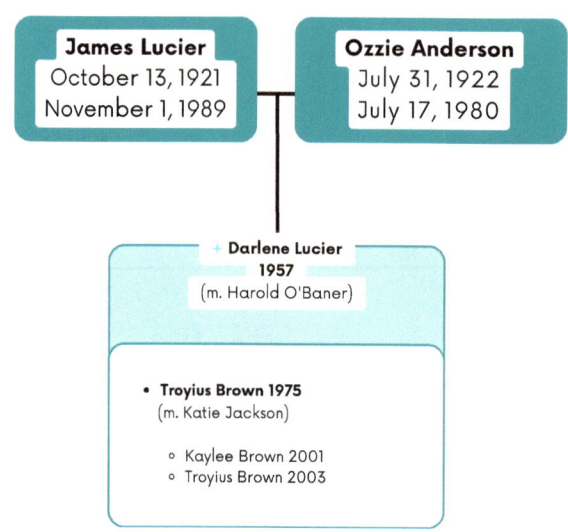

+ Non-Biological Child

2nd Born

William Lucier

William Lucier was born on June 13, 1923, in Williamson, Georgia, the second child of Henry T. and Ethel Lucier. From a young age, William demonstrated courage. When he was just a boy, he saved his newborn sister, Jeanette, from a house fire started by his brother Hermon. William carried his sister out of the burning home, placed her safely in a shed filled with corn husks, and then ran through the fields to alert his mother. This early act of bravery foreshadowed and define his life.

According to personal accounts, growing up in the racially segregated South, he often played with friends, including a few white boys, which was uncommon for the time. He was a skilled fist-fighter who never backed down from a challenge, whether in a friendly spar or a serious confrontation. He never lost either.

In his early years, William worked as a farmhand, with the 1940 U.S. Census listing his occupation as "Farm Hands, General Farm." He also worked in Ohio and Florida, traveling with a man named "Mr. Milt." Around the age of 18, William was hired by the railroad after being inspired by friends who were already employed in the industry. This marked the beginning of a long career with the railroad.

Born June 13, 1923
Died December 14, 2015
Buried Corinth Baptist Church, Rover, Georgia

Signal Corps

Private William Lucier

UNITES STATES ARMY

Ethel Kate Jones

Birth June 1, 1919
Death December 4, 2014

On March 13, 1942, William enlisted in the U.S. Army as a Private in Pike County, Georgia. He completed his training at Fort Benning and served as a communications specialist during World War II. His role involved maintaining and repairing critical communication lines essential for military operations. Following his military discharge, William returned to his job with the Southern Railroad Company. He worked on the "M" line, a route famously used by President Franklin D. Roosevelt during his trips to Warm Springs, Georgia. William dedicated 43 years to the railroad, excluding his time in the military, and became a respected figure in his field.

In 1946, William married Ethel Kate Jones. He had nine children, and the couple shared eight together. The family moved from Williamson to Griffin, Georgia, where William raised his children with unwavering dedication and love.

William Lucier passed away peacefully on December 14, 2015, at the age of 92. He was the longest-living child of Henry T. and Ethel Lucier. William's legacy continues to inspire those who knew him, reflecting a life well-lived and a character of remarkable happiness, big smiles and, grudge-free love.

Children:
Carolyn Lucier
Ruby Jewel Lucier
William Lucier Jr.
Lacy Lucier
Pinkey Lucier
Vanessa Lucier
Dora Lucier
Don Lucier
Ramon Jones

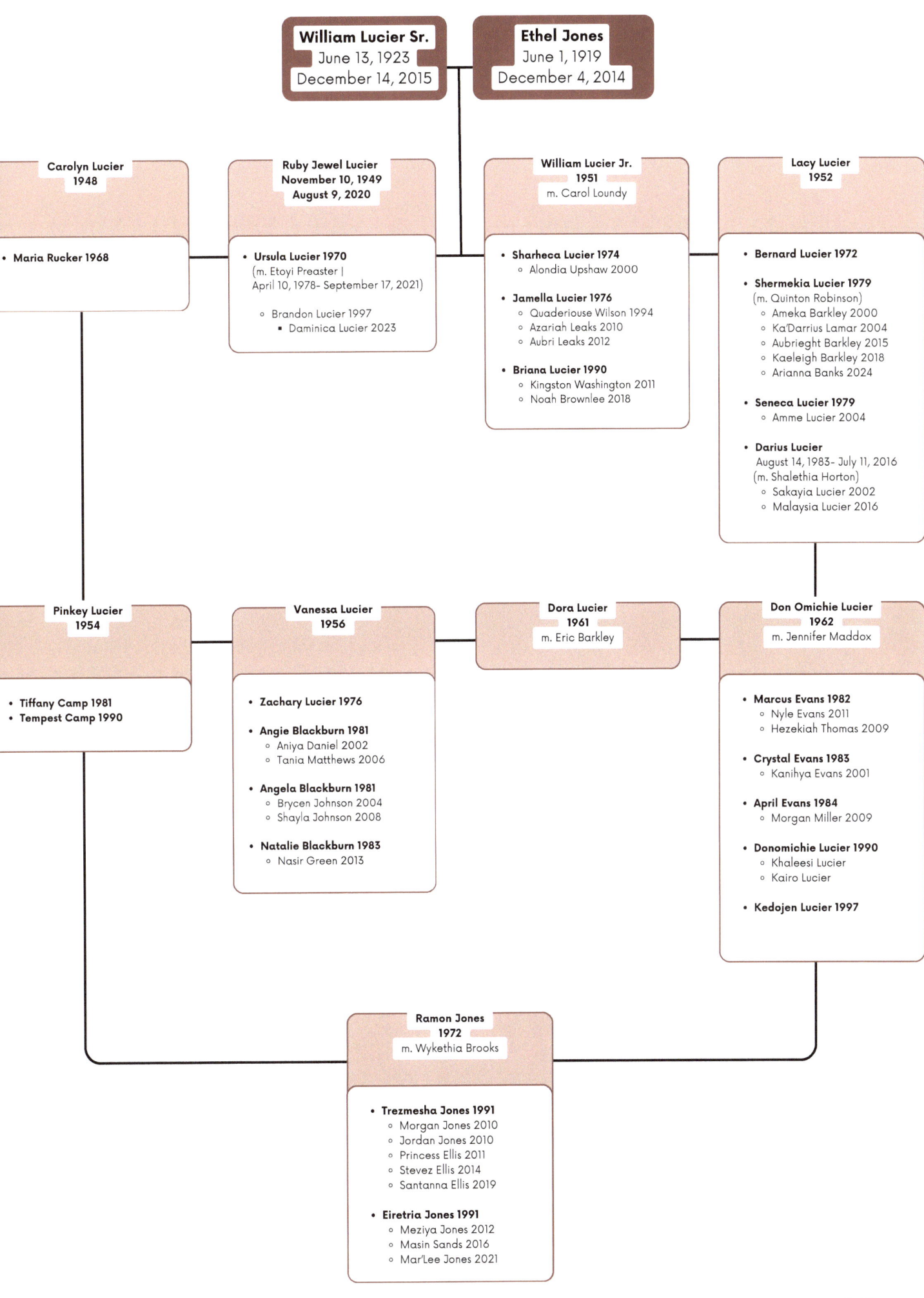

3rd Born

Catherine Lucier Livatt

Catherine Lucier Livatt, affectionately known as Cat, was born on August 3, 1925, in Rover, Georgia. She was the firstborn daughter of Henry T. Lucier, 29, and Ethel Lucier, 24. Cat's education ended after the 7th grade, but her intelligence and determination were evident throughout her life.

As a young adult, Cat worked as a housekeeper for R. Preston and Edna Bunn and their family in Griffin, Georgia. The Bunns, who later owned Bunn's Dry Cleaners- the oldest family-owned and operated dry cleaning business in Griffin- welcomed Cat into their home on High Falls Road. Her close relationship with the Bunn family was marked by mutual respect and affection, and she became so cherished that she was listed as a member of their household in the 1950 Census.

After leaving Griffin, Cat moved to Miami, Florida, where she lived with her husband, "LG." She later settled in Rochester, New York, where she entered into a common-law marriage with Edgar Sutton, affectionately known as "Uncle Slick." Cat's nurturing spirit extended beyond her immediate family, as she raised Grover Zachary and Rochelle Oliver as her own children.

Born August 3, 1925
Died August 23, 1989
Buried Mt. Hope Cemetary, Rochester, New York (site BB346z4)

Levin Grant "LG" Livatt

Birth July 18, 1919
Death May 28, 1989

"Cat"

Reared:
+ Grover Zachary
+ Rochelle Oliver

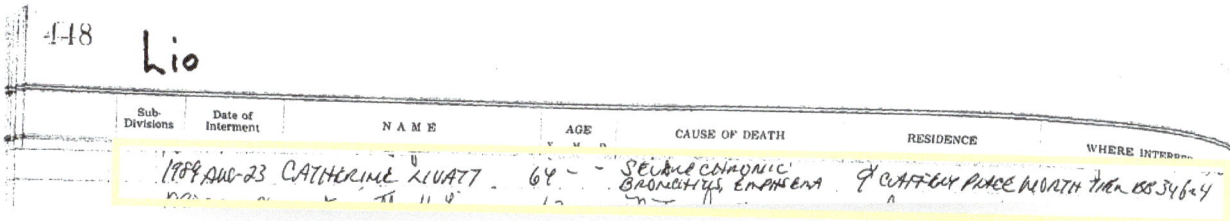

Throughout her later years, Cat battled chronic bronchitis and emphysema. She worked closely with pulmonary specialists in Rochester, earning their admiration for her resilience and determination. One doctor was so impressed by her character that he hired her while continuing to provide care. Despite her strength, Cat succumbed to severe bronchitis and emphysema in 1989 at the age of 64, shortly after returning from a family reunion in Georgia.

Her common-law husband, Uncle Slick, was devastated by her passing and reached out to her family with the bad news. The Lucier family traveled from Georgia and gathered in Rochester to honor her memory, with her nephews ensuring she was laid to rest with dignity. Cat's bond with her great-nephew, Cameron Oliver, Rochelle's firstborn, was particularly special. At just four years old, Cameron was by her side during her final moments, a testament to the love and connection she fostered within her family. Cat's life and legacy remain cherished by those who knew and loved her.

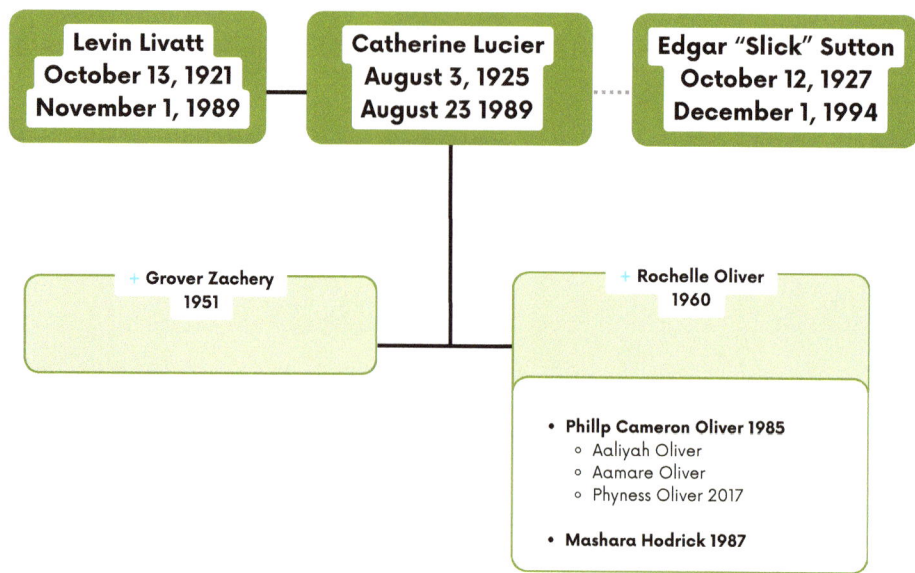

4th Born

Hermon Lucier

Hermon Lucier was born on May 7, 1927, in Rover, Georgia, as the fourth child of Ethel and Henry Lucier. From a young age, Hermon demonstrated a strong work ethic, beginning his career with the railroad, following in his father's footsptep's at just 12 years old.

During his early years, Hermon worked for Roy Buchanan, further honing his skills and work ethic. When he was mandated to register for World War II, Hermon followed the draft process but did not serve. Instead, he chose to remain in Williamson, Georgia, to support his mother, Ethel, after the passing of his father. As a newly widowed woman, Ethel lived with Hermon for a time before moving in with her youngest daughter, Josephine, to assist her family.

Hermon married Viola "Nina" on April 7, 1956. He was the father of six children and together they shared five children. As a member of the Railroad Extra Gang, Hermon contributed to laying tracks and expanding the railway system until his retirement. He worked diligently throughout his life, missing only one day in his 38-year career to celebrate Valentine's Day with his true love, "Iris" Viola.

Born May 7, 1927
Died July 29, 1995
Buried Free Liberty UMC, Williamson, Georgia

Viola Mahone

Birth June 3, 1935
Death November 11, 2007

Children: Jesse Marshall, Mary Lucier, Hermon Lucier Jr., Carol Lucier, Phyllis Lucier, Donna Lucier

Hermon Lucier was a cherished figure in the Williamson community, known for his wisdom and integrity. His front porch became a place of refuge for many, where everyone, regardless of race, was welcomed with words of wisdom, and offered a good drink of liquor, cold soda, and a little meat and bread from the kitchen.

Hermon was widely respected for his honesty and discretion. He frequently loaned, and sometimes gave, money to family and community members in need. He was also known for driving people where they needed to go, often at no charge, regardless of the distance. Hermon stood firm in his values, always upholding the truth and serving as a pillar of strength and generosity in his community.

Hermon Lucier passed away at the age of 68 in Decatur, Georgia. He was laid to rest at Free Liberty Methodist Church in Williamson, leaving behind a legacy of hard work, family devotion, and unwavering community service.

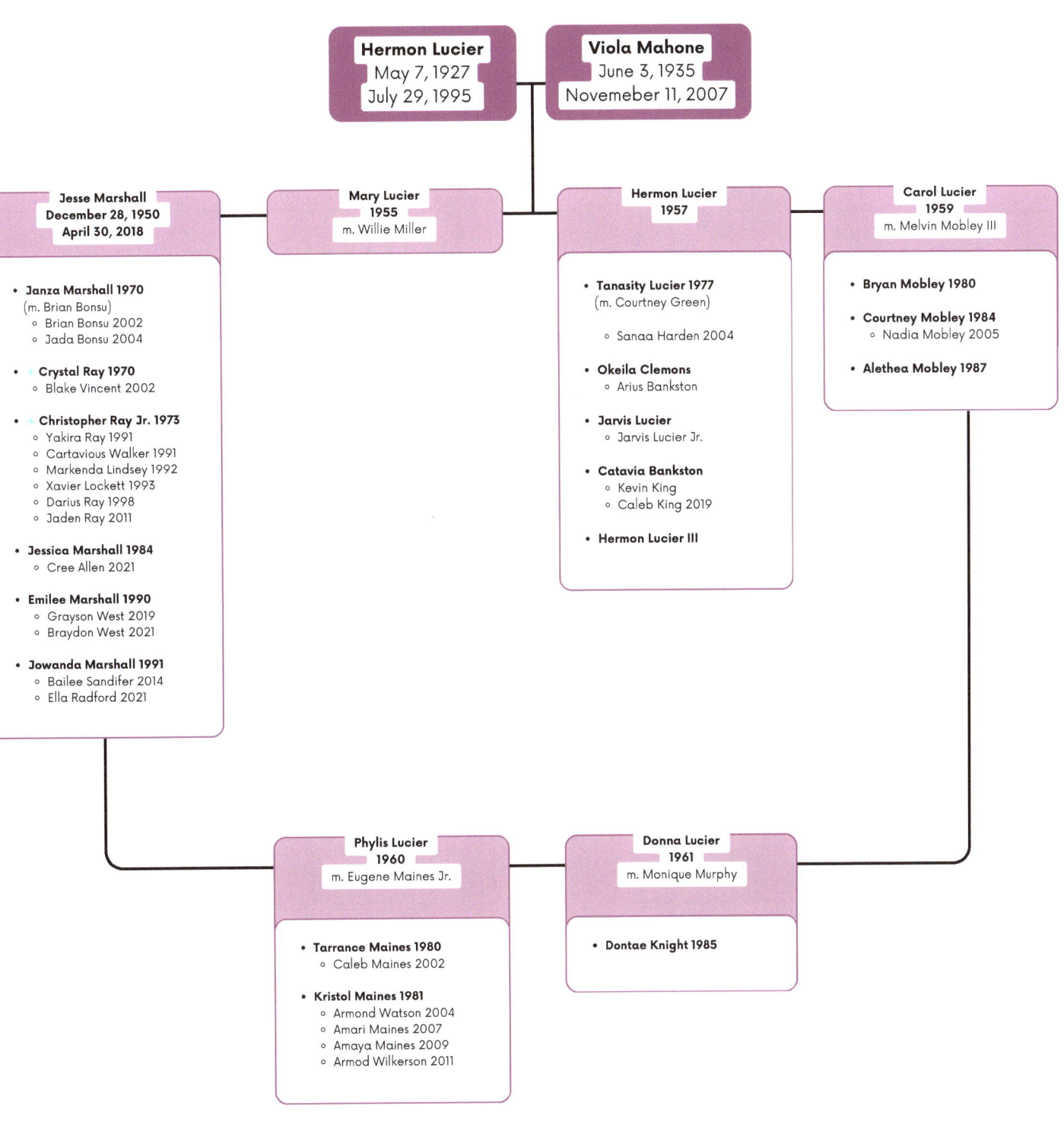

151

5th Born

Sarah Lucier Starks

Born in Williamson, Georgia, Ludie Sarah Lucier Starks was the second-born daughter of Ethel and Henry T. Lucier, arriving just ten days before her sister Eleanor Floyd. She was married to Willie J. Starks Sr., with whom she shared a life of devotion and eight children. Sarah was preceded in death by her first and second-born daughters and her husband, Willie, lovingly known as "Honey Boy."

In her early years, Sarah worked as a housekeeper at the Hilley's Home, later advancing her career as a Certified Nursing Assistant (CNA) at the Living Center Retirement Home.

Beyond her professional life, Sarah married Willie James, a preacher and entrepreneur who owned a store and social venue known for leisure and gaming. Willie James also earned recognition as the first- and at one time, only- Black American school bus driver in Pike County, Georgia.

"Muh"

Born April 20, 1929
Died April 9, 2013
Buried Free Liberty UMC, Williamson, Georgia

Willie James Starks Sr.

Birth December 23, 1924
Death March 27, 2008

Children:
Patricia Starks, Linda Starks, Samuel Starks, William Starks Jr., Richard Starks, Joe Starks, Cynthia Starks, Russell Starks

Reared:
+ Lutricia Starks, +Anthony Marshall and +Marc Crawley Jr.

To her children, Sarah was affectionately called "Muh," while her grandchildren lovingly recall her working tirelessly for minimum wages yet managing to provide high-dollar birthday gifts and cook meals abundant enough to feed an army weekly. Known for her love of Coca-Cola and her open-door hospitality, Sarah's home was a warm refuge for family members who wanted to visit. She also raised two of her grandsons and one granddaughter, Lutricia Starks, Anthony Marshall and Marc Crawley Jr., as her own.

Sarah outlived all of her siblings except her brother William and passed away on April 20, 2019, just days before her 84th birthday, following a courageous battle with cancer. She leaves behind a legacy of love, and unwavering devotion to her family.

Willie James Starks Sr.
December 23, 1924
March 27, 2008

Sarah Lucier
April 20, 1929
April 9, 2019

Patricia Starks
May 18, 1949
March 15, 2004
m. William Collier

- **Terrell Collier 1969**
  - Kimari Collier 1991
    - Deandre Donald Jr. 2019
  - Terrell Collier Jr. 1994
    - Kinsley Collier 2018
    - Keyston Collier 2020
  - Nicholes Collier 1997
- **Marcy Collier 1971**
  (m. Vincent Blackmon)
  - Brittany Gary 1995
    - Jordan Gary 2015
    - Khan Menton 2020
    - Kace Menton 2022
  - Leah Blackmon 2002

Linda Starks
June 25, 1950
December 4, 2004
m. Virgil Crawley

- **Lutricia Starks 1966**
  - D'Amani Dillahunty 1996
    - Alaiya Dillahunty 2022
  - D'Mylo Dillahunty 2001
- **Anthony Marshall 1968**
  (m. Carolyn Smith)
  - Lonesha Polk Marshall 1991
    - Nikhia Newsome 2008
    - Da' Monie Barconey 2011
    - Da' Mya Barconey 2012
    - De' Lani Morris 2016
    - Dontre Morris Jr. 2018
    - D' iona Morris 2023
  - Anthony Marshall Jr.
    - Ahking Marshall 2012
    - Ethan Marshall 2014
    - Kynlee Marshall 2016
    - Zaidyn Marshall 2018
    - Aubrielle Marshall 2022
    - Truth Marshall 2023
  - Tyjae Marshall 1994
    - India Marshall 2020
    - Trenton Marshall 2022
- **Marc Crawley 1969**
  (m. Lisa Talley)
  - Marc Crawley II 1992
    (m. Aminah Flowers)
    - Yasmeen Crawley 2019
    - Asiyah Crawley 2024
  - Marquise Crawley 1996

Samuel Starks
1951
m. Lisa Drag

- **Terrance Wright 1974**
- **Keene Starks 1974**
  (m. Jeffery Wright)
  - Jamal Wright 1997
  - Jordan Samuel Wright 2001
- **Bettina Starks 1976**
  (m. Donzell Bland)
  - Carlton Watson 1991
  - Toni McGowan 1994
  - Brittani McGowan 1998
  - Zaria Bland 2009
  - Legacy Bland 2015
  - Legend Bland
  April 07, 2015-January 21, 2015
- **Rashard Starks**
  November 11, 1980
  September 1, 2012
  (m. Angel Webb)
  - Makayla Starks 2008
- **Omah Starks 1983**
  - Shykeiria Starks 2001
    - Nikolai Starks 2024
  - Omah Levi Jabez Starks 2015
  - Omarion Starks 2016
- **Jabril Starks**
  - Jolanda Starks 2009
  - Cayden Starks 2012
  - Heaven Starks 2022
- **Laquita Starks 1993**
  - Kendall Starks 2012
  - Kehlani Coleman 2017
  - Khali Coleman 2021

Willie James Starks Jr.
1952
m. Ann

- **Nikki Starks 1975**
  - Ariele Dorsey
    - Aydin Dickson 2010
    - Alivia Dorsey 2018
  - Jalen Starks 2011
    - Emmerie Starks 2021
- **Marcus Starks 1983**
  - D'Corian Starks 2008
  - Ny' Asia Starks 2009
  - Kailee Day 2016

Richard Starks I
1953
m. Lena Williams

- **Kandice Starks 1980**
  - Victor Cheeves
  - Kamryn Cheeves I
    - Kamryn Cheeves II
  - Kaleb Cheeves
  - Kaden Cheeves
- **Kirby Starks 1984**
- **Richard Starks II 1990**
  - Ryan Starks 2009
  - Yalyn Starks 2009
  - Jariah Starks 2010
  - Austin Starks 2011
  - Kaci Starks
  - Kari Starks
  - Konnor Starks
  - Kati Starks

Joe Scott Starks
1956
m. Marsha

- **Joel Starks Sr. 1973**
  (m. Demetrice McCune)
  - Deonte Lanier
  - Josiah Starks
  - Joel Starks Jr.
  - Aaliyah Starks
- **Kenithia Starks 1975**
  - Leon Starks 2005
  - Autum Colquitt
- **Rain Shalom (Tonya Starks) 1979**
  (m. Ras Na'seekh Shalom)
  - Toni Murrieta 1997
    - Jayden Gonzalez
    - Jordan Gonzalez
    - Gianna Gonzalez
  - Arin Murrieta 1998
    - A'lanni Gilbert 2020
  - JaQuavious Starks 2002
  - Devyn Yarbrough 2003
  - Jah' Karia Yarbrough 2023
  - Joseph Yarbrough 2005
- **Dominique Forts 1994**
  - Ayden Forts 2013

Cynthia Starks
1958
m. Kenneth Smith

- **Kenneth Reid Jr.**
  - Angelina Reid
    (m. Jacoby Weston)
    - Kynlee Weston
    - Nalaya Conway
  - LyKera Reid
  - Kentavious Reid
  - Kendarious Reid
- **Kentrell Reid**
  - Sa'riah Smith 2000
    - Aalireva Jester 2018
  - Aazani Boone
  - Dais'ya Reid
  - Ry' Qaureona Reid
- **O' Kendrick Reid 1979**
  (m. Tyeisha Reid)
  (m. Kristie Reid- deceased)
  - Taisean Reid 1998
  - Kelis Reid 2001
    - Gruenely Reid
  - Kahliyah Reid 2001
    - Judah David
    - Cairo David
  - Saron Reid 2006

Russell Starks
1959
m. Grace Passmore

- **Ericka Starks 1980**
  - Jaknylah Barkley 2003
    - Stormii Stargell 2024
  - JaKylei Horton 2020
- **Tiana Starks 1984**
  - Zadiah Freeman 2004
    - August Thomas 2024
  - Quran Wright 2007
  - Jay Wright 2009
- **Annisia Starks 1986**
  - London Evans 2002
  - Arkeyveon Starks 2006

6th Born

Eleanor Floyd Houston

Eleanor Jean Floyd was born on April 30, 1929, to Ophelia Pate Floyd and Henry T. Lucier. Although Henry T. Lucier was her biological father, Eleanor grew up knowing Louis Floyd, her mother's husband, as her father. Louis had passed away in 1928, before her birth.

Eleanor spent her early years in Thomaston, Georgia, before relocating to Columbus, Ohio. There, she lived at 673 East Engler Street. Eleanor and Johnnie B. Houston's love story began at the corner of Engler Street and Seymour Avenue in Columbus, where they started as neighbors. Their friendship grew into a deep love, culminating in their marriage on September 4, 1946.

Together, they built a lifelong partnership and went on to raise seven children together.

Throughout her career, Eleanor worked as an inspector at Ross Labs until her retirement. She was also a devoted member of the Corinthian Baptist Church.

Born April 30, 1929
Died February 19, 1993
Buried Green Lawn Cemetary, Columbus, Ohio

Johnnie B. Houston
Birth March 12, 1925
Death November 19, 2000

"Jean"

Children:
Faithe Houston
Venida Houston
John Houston
Silas Houston
William Houston
Margaretta Houston
Cary Houston-Bolden

For much of her life, Henry T. Lucier's other children were unaware of Eleanor's existence. It wasn't until 1980 that they finally met her. They immediately began immersing themselves into getting to know each other and seamlessly adding to life together.

Through hard work and determination, Eleanor saved enough to purchase her first home at 1471 E. 21st Avenue in Columbus. This home became a sanctuary for her family, a place where love thrived and generations gathered. Today, the home remains in the family, a lasting testament to Eleanor's dedication and the strong foundation she built for her loved ones.

Eleanor passed away in 1993 at the age of 64. She was laid to rest in Green Lawn Cemetary in Columbus, Ohio. Coincidentally, it is the same cemetery her great-uncle Fletcher, was buried, who she never knew existed, and who had raised his family in Franklin, Ohio till death. His descendants along with hers still greatly reside within the area.

156

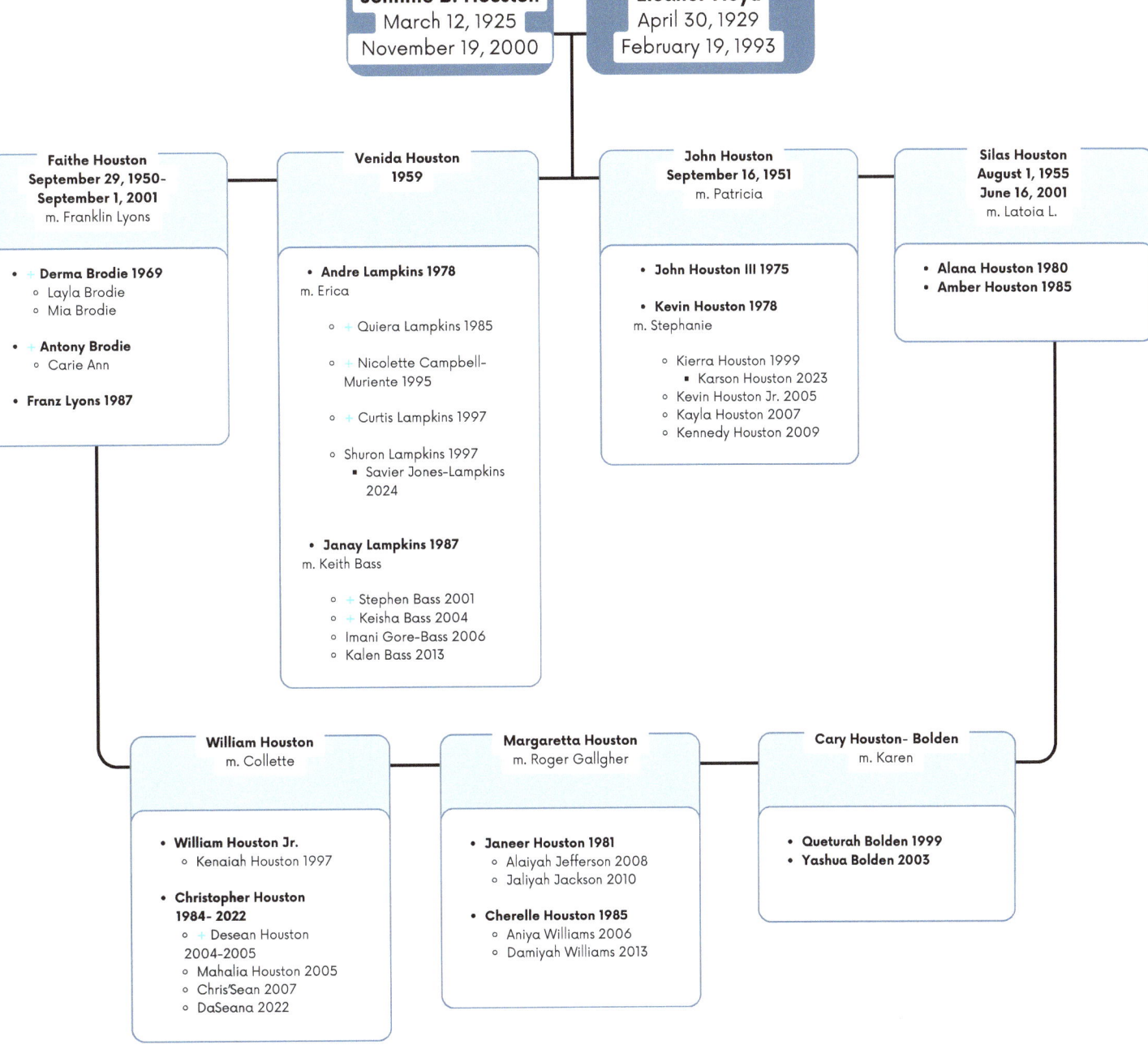

7th Born

Ben Lucier

Born October 1930
Died May 18, 1931
Buried Free Liberty AM Church, Williamson, GA

Ben Lucier, the seventh child of Henry T. and Ethel Lucier, lived a brief but cherished life. He passed away at just seven months old due to complications from pleurisy and pneumonia, which ultimately led to heart failure.

Today, his resting place lies in the Free Liberty Family Cemetery, beside his mother's grave. Though his grave remains unmarked, his memory endures as a poignant reminder of his family's love and loss.

8th Born

Jeanette Lucier Starks

Abbey Jeanette Lucier Starks was born on March 29, 1932, in Rover, Georgia, to Henry T. and Ethel Lucier. She married Robert Starks Sr., a preacher and truck driver, in Griffin, Georgia. Together, they raised eight children. Robert later worked at Ford Motor Company, where he built cars before retiring to focus on preaching.

In her early years, Jeanette worked as a Certified Nursing Assistant (CNA) at the Living Center Nursing Home. She also served as a domestic worker for Harold and Mickey Shepherd and as a babysitter at First Presbyterian Church. She eventually left her job at the church to work at Rushton Cotton Mill.

In 1975, after years of hard work, Robert retired Jeanette from her job. She decided she'd learn to drive a car, but ultimately never drove and depended on her husband Robert to chauffer her around town. A responsibility that he obliged happily.

Born March 29, 1932
Died September 13, 2008
Buried Free Liberty UMC Church, Williamson, GA

"Jenny Belle"

Robert Lewis Starks Sr.

Birth September 11, 1930
Death November 11, 2011

STARKS
LYDIA CELITHA
AUG. 10, 1960
MAR. 27, 1970

9-Year-Old Dies In Fire

Little Miss Lydia Celitha "Lisa" Starks, nine-year-old daughter of the Rev. and Mrs. Robert Starks of Williamson, burned to death Friday night when the Stark home was destroyed by fire.

She was a fourth grade student at Pike County Elementary School in Zebulon.

In addition to her parents, she is survived by two sisters, Shirley Starks and Kathy Starks, both of Williamson; five brothers, Robert Starks Jr., James Harold Starks, Danny Starks, all of California, Mitchell Gerald Starks and Christopher Starks, both of Williamson; grandmothers, Mrs. Ethel Lucier of Williamson and Mrs. Mattie Starks of Locust Grove.

Funeral services will be conducted Tuesday afternoon at 2 o'clock from the Free Liberty Metodist Church in Williamson. The Rev. O. B. Boone, The Rev. W. H. Stephens and the Rev. J. H. Johnson will officiate and burial will be in the church cemetery. Miller Funeral Home is in charge of plans.

The Stark family is residing with Mrs. Josephine Reid of Williamson, sister of Mrs. Stark.

Children:
Robert Starks Jr.
James Harold Starks
Danny Starks
Shirley Starks
Mitchell Starks
Christopher Starks
Kathy Starks
Lydia Starks

Reared:
+Jacqueline Starks

Jeanette's life was marked by both profound love and devastating tragedy. In 1970, the Starks family faced a life-altering event when their home was set on fire by what has been believed to be by a group of racist white men. While their sons managed to escape, their youngest daughter, Lydia, affectionately known as "Lisa," was pulled from the burning house unresponsive and did not survive. This heartbreaking loss was not the first time fire had shaped Jeanette's life. As a baby, her childhood home in Rover, Georgia, was reportedly set ablaze. Later, her eldest daughter suffered severe burns in a fire at the age of three. The family had already endured two house fires before the tragic loss of Lisa, leaving a lasting impact on their lives.

Despite these hardships, Jeanette and Robert remained devoted to their surviving children. Their family grew when they took in Jacqueline Starks, the daughter of their son James Harold, from California. They raised Jacqueline as their own, making her the ninth child in the Starks household.

Later in life, Jeanette realized that many of the community children and adults had not ever left their township. She began organizing trips to concerts, Six Flags, White Waters and jazz festivals for the adults.

Jeanette passed away in 2008 at the age of 76 due to a massive heart attack. Her life was defined by resilience, dedication to her family, and unwavering strength in the face of adversity.

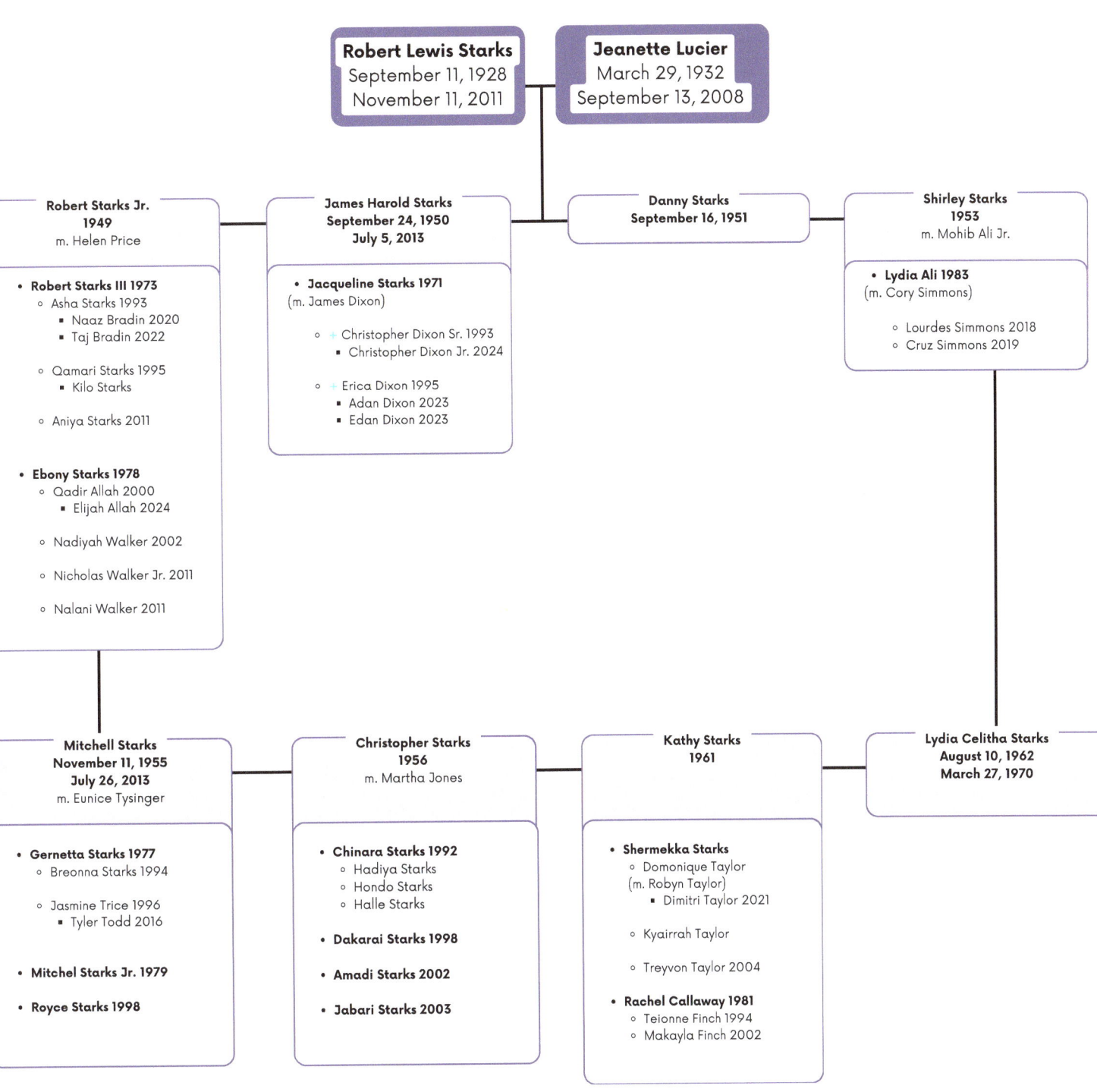

9th Born

Josephine Lucier Reid

Josephine Lucier Reid was born on October 11, 1933, in Williamson, Georgia, the youngest daughter of Ethel and Henry T. From an early age, Josie displayed determination qualities that would shape her journey through life.

As a young woman, Josie married Roger Reid, and together they built a family, welcoming six children: Winfred, Dorothy, Roger Jr., David, Rickey, and Grant Reid. Josie and Margie Battle was known in the community as being the coordinators of the Easter program at Free Liberty, Antioch and Chapel Hill Church.

To support their growing household, Josie worked tirelessly as a housemaid, first for Miller Patton and later for Johnny and Velma Killingsworth. Her dedication and the strong relationships she built with her employers became evident in the trust they placed in her. Johnny Killingsworth, recognizing her commitment, allowed Josie and her husband Roger to use his car on weekends to run errands and manage family affairs.

Born October 11, 1933
Died March 3, 1978
Buried Free Liberty UMC Church, Williamson, GA

"Josie"

Roger Reid Sr.

Birth May 6, 1932
Death November 12, 1961

Tragedy struck during one such weekend in an event that would change Josie's life forever. While driving the borrowed car, Roger was involved in a devastating accident that left the vehicle wrecked and claimed his life. At just 29 years old, Roger's neck was broken in the crash, leaving Josie widowed with six young children to raise on her own.

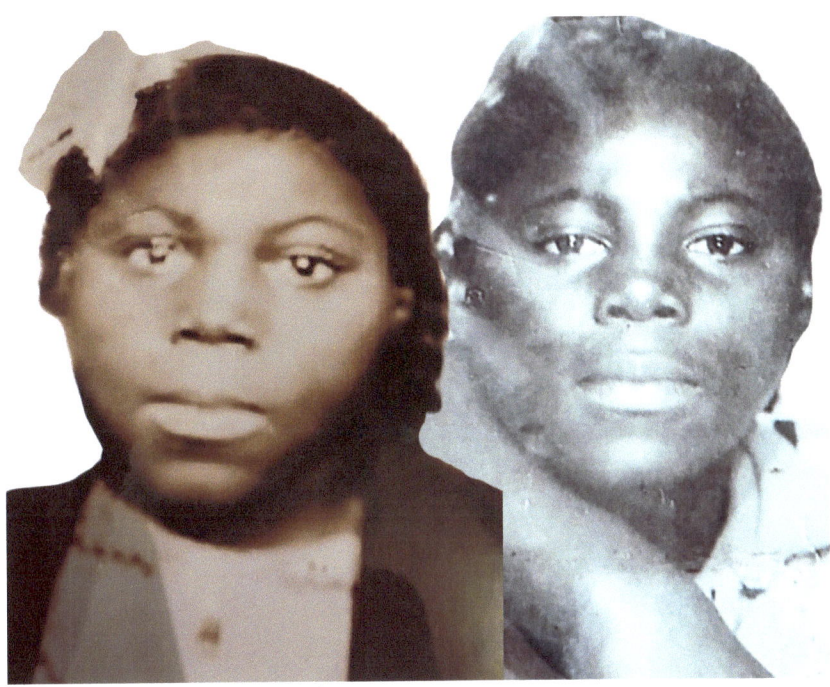

Undeterred by hardship, Josie continued to work to support her family. Before her health declined, she took a job at United Cotton Goods, a role that showcased her determination to provide for her children despite the challenges she faced. She even taught Jeanette to drive. But we have come to know that despite Josie's efforts, Jeanette did not drive.

Later in life, Josie was diagnosed with Crohn's disease, an illness that brought its own set of difficulties. Her battle with the disease ultimately led to her untimely death in 1978.

Josie's life, though marked by profound loss and adversity, stands as a testament to her strength, love, and commitment to her family. Her legacy lives on through her children and the enduring memories of her perseverance.

Children:
Winfred Reid
Dorothy Reid
Roger Reid Jr.
David Reid
Rickey Reid
Grant Reid

Roger Reid Sr.
May 6, 1932
November 12, 1961

Josephine Lucier
October 11, 1933
March 3, 1978

Winfred Reid Sr.
1948

- **Winfred Reid Jr. 1975**
  - Jalon Reid 1999
  - Jordan Reid 2006
- **Rashad Shoats 1983**
  (m. Shay Middlebrooks)
  - Jordan Shoats 2004
  - Jaeden Shoats 2007
  - Madison Shoats 2014
  - Isaac Shoats 2017
- **Sharmal Monquaze Reid**
  August 24, 1989
  April 6, 2021

Dorothy Reid
June 11, 1950
October 9, 2020

- **Leslie Reid 1971**
- **LaToya Reid**
  October 31, 1984
  August 22, 2017
  - Jamir Reid 2002
  - Katori Evans 2004
    - Ryder Evans 2025
  - Tyler Reid 2008

Roger Reid Jr.
1953
m. Lois Ogletree

- **Roydric Reid 1974**
  - Schylur Reid 1997
  - Roydric Reid Jr. 2009
  - Amy Reid 2002
  - Khloe Reid 2017
  - Kaythan Reid 2018
- **Debrea Reid 1977**
  - Nahja Stodghill 2002
- **+ Alexis Ogletree 1982**
  - TJ Barlow 1998
    - Afyinti Barlow 2019
    - Aaliyah Barlow 2021
    - Addison Barlow 2023
  - Tkai Ogletree 2002
  - Tabiys Ogletree 2004

David Reid
1954
m. Gwendolyn Marshall

- **+ Rontea Marshall 1979**
  - Rontea Stevens 2007
  - Mya Stevens 2006
- **Ashley Reid 1985**

Rickey Reid
1955
m. Linda Clemmons

- **Fredrick Perdue 1972**
  - Jasmine Perdue 1997
    - Marley Perdue 2019
  - Emoni Perdue 1997
  - Ski Perdue 2000
- **Ormetra Reid**
  April 4, 1976
  August 7, 2000
- **+ Markita Starks 1989**
  - Markevious Starks 2007
  - Za'Rayia Starks 2008
  - Martayvious Starks 2009
  - Sincere Starks 2012
  - Aiden Starks 2013

Grant Reid
January 1, 1962
February 18, 2012

- **Reginald Reid 1982**
  (m. Lakeisha Reid)
  - Gi'quain Crawford 2000
  - Regiyun Reid 2007
  - Uzziahn Reid 2008
  - Armoni Reid 2011
  - Isreal Crawford 2023
- **Gaylen Reid 1983**
  - Ti'Amari Reid 2003

+ Non-Biological Child

10th Born

Born May 17, 1937
Died December 24, 2004
Buried Free Liberty UMC, Williamson, Georgia

Lourdes Bantugan Lucier

Birth February 10, 1952

Josiah Lucier

Josiah L. Lucier, born on May 17, 1937, in Williamson, Georgia, was the tenth child of Henry T. and Ethel Lucier, who was 41 years old at the time of his birth. He married Mariam Walker and Dorothy Evans, with whom he had six children. In 1991, he wed Lourdes Bantugan, who supported him through complications of diabetes until his passing.

Throughout his military service, Josiah held the rank of Hospitalman Second Class in the U.S. Navy during the Vietnam War. Fondly referred to as "Doc" Lucier, he gained recognition for his compassionate medical care, especially towards Vietnamese villagers and children.

In 1965, LIFE magazine featured him in a photo essay that showcased his unwavering dedication amidst the brutal realities of war.

"The Doc"

Hospitalman Second Class

UNITED STATES NAVY

After his military service, Josiah joined a Vietnam veterans treatment program at the VA hospital in Menlo Park, California. He was featured in the 1982 KRON documentary The War Within, which highlighted the impact of PTSD on Vietnam veterans.

Lucier became a key figure in military PTSD research, much like Henrietta Lacks in medical science. His case contributed to studies at the Uniformed Services University and Walter Reed, helping to advance trauma treatment for service members. His participation helped shape modern PTSD therapies used in military mental health care today.

Josiah L. Lucier passed away on December 24, 2004, at age 67. He was laid to rest at Free Liberty United Methodist Church Cemetery in Williamson, Georgia. His contributions continue to influence PTSD treatment for veterans and inspire compassionate medical assistance throughout war services.

Children:
Leonardo Lucier, Carlon Lucier, Zandra Lucier, Vincent Lucier, Scott Lucier, Marc Lucier

In March 1965, 3,500 U.S. Marines landed in South Vietnam. By year's end, there were 200,000 of them. When LIFE dispatched Associate Editor Michael Mok and Photographer Paul Schutzer to spend six weeks with them, the two men found the Marines mired in a world of ambiguity: They were at once dispatching lives and saving them, hailed as heroes and decried as villains.

Mok and Schutzer risked their lives to bring LIFE's readers a 22-page photo essay on the "blunt reality" of the war—one that, Mok wrote, vividly called to mind scenes from Saipan in World War II and Inchon in the Korean War. "Only the locale is different, and this observer, now a generation older. No one used to call him 'Pop' or 'Sir' in the old days."

The scenes the men captured, in images and words, reflect a world in which bullets and bandages were doled out in equal measure. The Marines carried out their missions, killing and capturing Viet Cong soldiers, but they also undertook a broader mission to win the hearts and minds of the people whose world they occupied. Treating the Vietnamese with dignity was as much a matter of human decency as it was a strategy to win the war: To acquire crucial intelligence from villagers, the Marines needed first to earn their trust.

The essay's most enduring images are not those that portray scenes of battle and warfare, but those that capture the humanity of people embroiled in a situation not of their own making. There's the Vietnamese mother carrying her wounded baby through her besieged village, and the U.S. Marine who scoops him up to get him to a medic, to no avail. There are Marines handing out dolls to children who have nothing, and children ripping them limb from limb, preferring the disembodied head of a doll to no doll at all.

The magazine chose a face to encapsulate the humanitarian side of American forces, and that face belonged to Hospitalman Second Class Josiah Lucier, 29. Nicknamed "The Doc," Lucier's primary job was to keep the Marines healthy. But, Mok wrote, "then there is the job he does because he *wants* to, which is holding sick call for all the villagers within walking distance." Lucier treated his patients, especially the children, with a tenderness that's palpable in photographs.

But he wasn't Pollyannaish about the world he'd been living in for three years. Lucier carried a gun when he made house calls, never knowing where the enemy lurked. "I am a humanitarian and all that jazz," he said, "but I am not completely out of my ever-lovin' mind."

For wartime readers, these images matched images of the faceless enemy with universal pictures of love and loss. They show another side to the soldier who might return home to be spit upon and scorned, a recipient of misplaced hatred.

The Marines, for their part, didn't need to be greeted with protest signs to grapple with the gray area in which they lived each day. They had already internalized it. Said one, "Sometimes I feel like one of the bad guys ... When we go into these *villes* and the people look at you in that sad kind of way they have, it's pretty hard for me to imagine I'm wearing a white hat and riding a white horse."

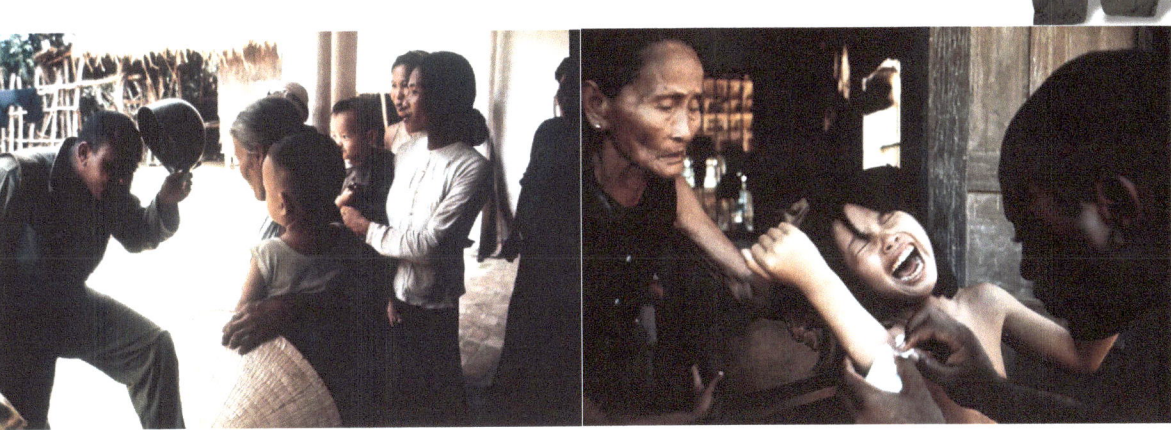

Caption from LIFE. On his self-appointed rounds, Hospitalman 2|c Josiah Lucier doffs his helmet liner to some of the villagers. Paul Schutzer – The LIFE Picture Collection/Getty Images

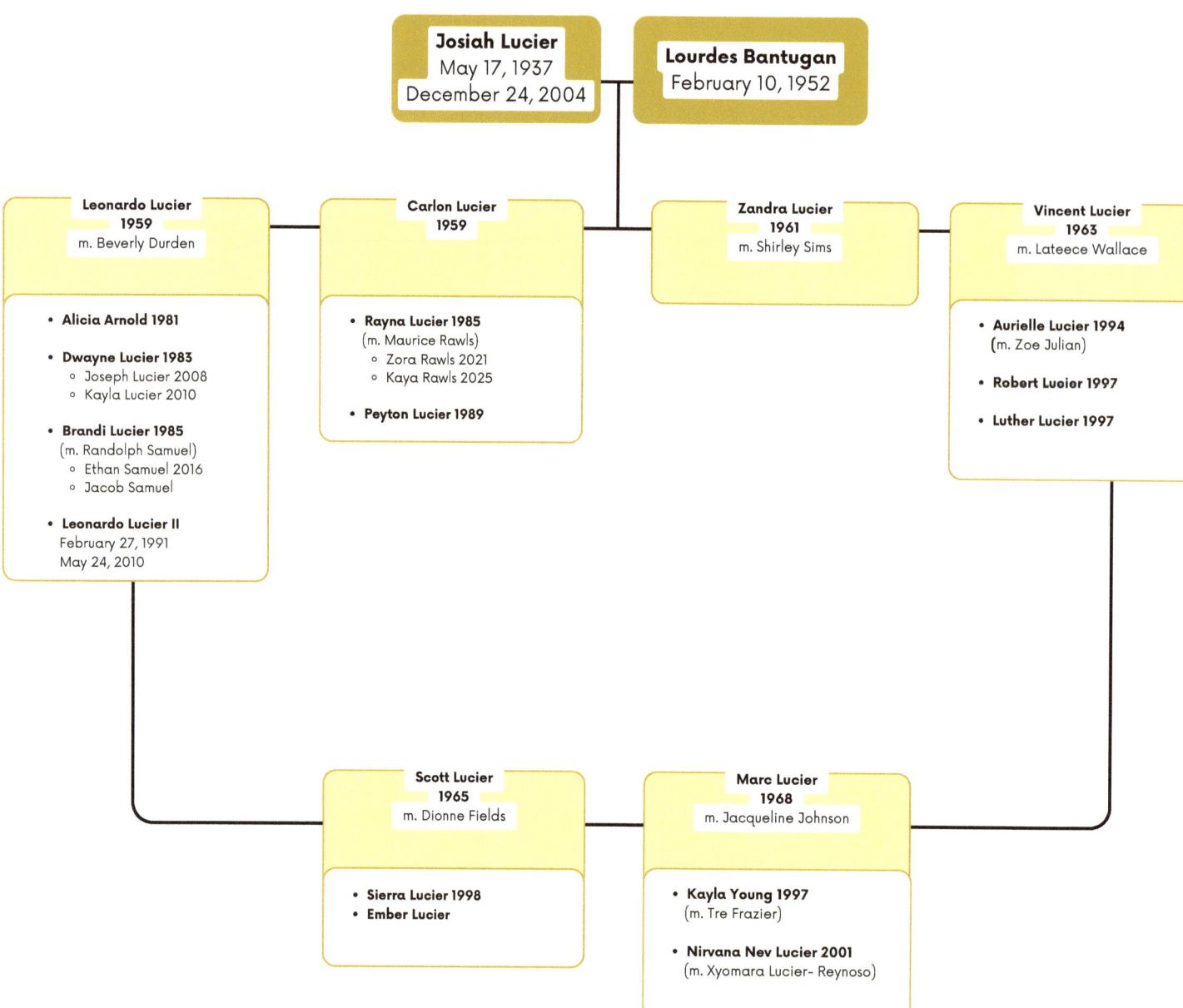

11th Born

Harold Ray Lucier

Harold Lucier was the 11th born and youngest child of Henry T. and Ethel Lucier. Tragically, his father, Henry, passed away just months before Harold was born. Raised by his widowed mother, Harold grew up with his older siblings and the children of Josie, Jeanette, and Sarah Lucier.

As a young man, Harold moved from Williamson to Atlanta, where he worked at a furniture store. Seeking new opportunities, he later traveled west to join his older brother, Josiah, in California. Harold embraced life on the West Coast, forming new connections and a vibrant social circle. Known by the CB handle "046," Harold was remembered for his outgoing personality and love of entertaining. Visitors often remarked that being around him felt like staying at a resort.

Harold married Betty Freeman, and together they became a family of three, raising Betty's son, Richard Calvin.

The couple later welcomed a daughter, Lakeisha, who became the youngest grandchild of Henry and Ethel Lucier.

Born January 19, 1939
Died June 17, 1995
Buried Free Liberty UMC, Williamson, Georgia

"046"

Betty Freeman Lucier

Birth October 16, 1937
Death December 7, 2018

Harold's nieces and nephews fondly recalled him as a beloved babysitter during their childhoods, describing him as "everyone's buddy" who brought joy and laughter wherever he went.

Harold passed away at the age of 56 in Santa Ana, California. His wife and children ensured his final wish was honored by bringing him back home to be buried alongside his family in Williamson, Georgia at Free Liberty Methodist Church.

Children:
+ Richard Calvin
Lakeisha Lucier

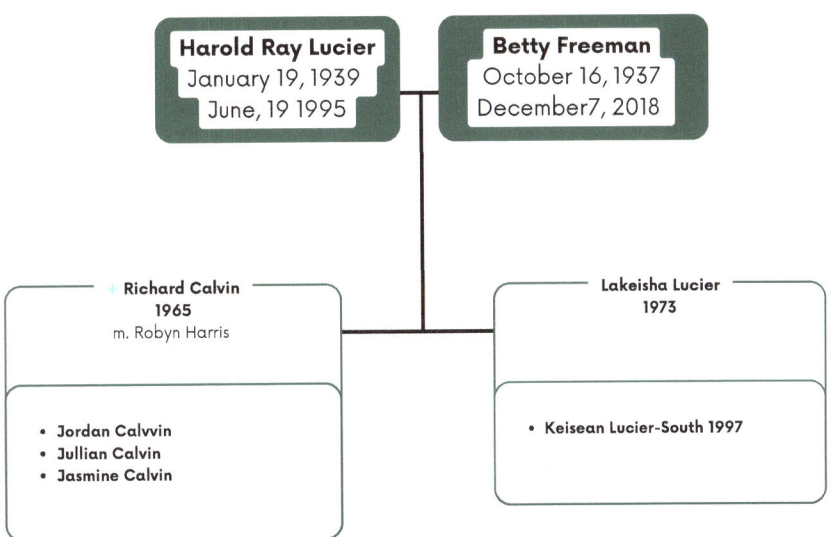

Harold Ray Lucier
January 19, 1939
June, 19 1995

Betty Freeman
October 16, 1937
December 7, 2018

+ Richard Calvin
1965
m. Robyn Harris

- Jordan Calvvin
- Jullian Calvin
- Jasmine Calvin

Lakeisha Lucier
1973

- Keisean Lucier-South 1997

+ Non-Biological Child

173

Adopted Daughter

Azzie Lee Marshall

Azzie Lee Crawford was born in 1927 to Limmie (Swann) Crawford and Henry Crawford. She married Joseph Marshall, affectionately known as "Uncle Toot," in Williamson, Georgia, where their daughter Anne Marshall Youngblood was born.

During her early years in Williamson, Azzie developed a close bond with Ethel Lucier and her daughters. She worked as a domestic housekeeper for Howard Connell, a local grocery owner, and for helping care for Ethel's young children. Over time, Azzie was lovingly embraced as the twelfth of Ethel's 11 children.

Azzie later moved to the Miami-Dade area in Florida, where she worked as a hairdresser for many years. She was the mother of one daughter, Diane Youngblood.

Azzie passed away at the age of 69 in Miami-Dade, Florida, and is buried at Dade Memorial Park in Opa-locka, Florida.

Born Dec 16, 1927
Died May 1, 1997
Buried Dade Memorial Park, Opa-locka, Florida

"Azalee"

Joseph "Toot" Marshall

Birth March 16, 1925
Death February 27, 2012

Children:
Diane Youngblood

175

Joseph Marshall
March 16, 1925
February 27, 2012

+ **Azzie Lee**
December 16, 1927
May 1, 1997

Dianne Marshall
November 10, 1954
m. Lyndell Youngblood

- **Theresa Youngblood**
- **Angie Youngblood**
- **Kim Youngblood**
- **Melissa Youngblood**

THE CHILDREN OF
HENRY T. LUCIER

LUCIER

FAMILY REUNION

LUCIER

LUCIER

Lucier- Lindsey Family Reunions

As the years went on, the Lucier family sought to reconnect and celebrate their shared history. After years of living distant from one another, they initiated a family reunion, a tradition that became a cornerstone of their story. The reunions were a time to see aging parents and siblings, welcome new generations of children, and come together as a community. Hundreds of family members traveled from New York, California, Florida, Ohio, Tennessee, and all over Georgia to participate in these multi-day celebrations. They gathered to eat, play, party, and reunite, creating memories that would last a lifetime.

The family reunions were spearheaded by Shirley Starks Ali, Jeanette Starks, and a dedicated committee of family and friends in 1988. Together, they organized donations, venues, travel accommodations, food, sponsorships, partnerships, music, attire, awards, giveaways, events, festivities and a homecoming celebration. For many years, these reunions were the only times the family gathered outside of funerals. Over time, as beloved family members and cornerstones of the family passed away, the reunions became a way to honor their legacy and celebrate the family's resilience and unity. In 1989, Will Lucier coordinated the second large- scale family reunion.

However, as the years progressed and loved ones were lost, the reunions gradually came to an end. On their grand scale, there hasn't been another family reunion since 1989. Today, the family celebrates together annually in a combined neighborhood block party shared with the residents of "Dark Town," past and present. The event is affectionately named the "Weesum Family Reunion" where a portion of Second District Road is occupied along with the properties of the residents on the same road for the day party and tailgate. In 2024, Lakeisha Lucier and Lynn Starks worked together to orchestrate a family reunion at Fairmount Park for the residents of Georgia. The event was a one-day park barbeque where the family was able to come together for food, drinks, pictures and to love on one another for a few hours. But, the passing of key family members marked the end of this cherished tradition, on a large scale- leaving behind memories of joy, connection, and unity. Despite this, the spirit of those gatherings lives on in the hearts of the Lucier descendants, reminding them of their shared heritage and the enduring strength of their family.

David Reid: Family Historian and Research Pioneer

To commemorate the family's earliest reunions, David Reid, the son of Josephine Lucier and Roger Reid, began the journey of documenting our family history back in the late 80's. At that time, genealogical filing systems were outdated, requiring significant effort to navigate between facilities to access microfilm and archives for gathering family information. Many of these documents were redacted, some were uncatalogued, and a lot simply weren't available to the public yet. There were no digital databases, internet findings nor platforms to connect DNA sampling. David worked to trace our lineage as far back as the information permitted by hand with "boots on the ground."

David was forced to stop his research after suffering multiple heart attacks and the work of this magnitude laid dormant for over 25 years. The efforts undertook in 2024 and 2025 to allocate resources and funding for the research that contributed to this book series builds upon his pioneering work in exploring the history of the Lucier family, first and foremost.

Below, you will find a visual representation of the original family tree created by David Reid, which illustrates the connections within the Lucier family and branches into the siblings of Ethel Lucier's family lineage. This tree was complemented by a video, also made by David Reid, that interweaved images and photographs of the family to showcase our lineage during that period. Many of the family also had the image screen printed onto t-shirts to wear the pride of our history.

We salute and pay homage to David Reid for laying the foundation of our work and research for today's discoveries.

David "Smoke" Reid | Photographer, Videographer, Historian, and Storyteller

Original Family Tree Visual, Created by David Reid

LUCIER

GRAND CHILDREN

LUCIER

LUCIER

The Dangers of the 1950's, 60's and beyond

From as early as the 1700s, the Lucier family has left an indelible mark on history, forging a legacy of strength and progress. Through the centuries, their journey has been marked by adversity, determination, and triumphs that reverberate across generations. This truth begins with Henry T. and Ethel Lucier, whose family survived and endured the trials of the Civil Rights Era in a Southern sundown town- a term that describes communities where African Americans were threatened with violence if found there after dark. Though the term "sundown town" wasn't widely recognized at the time, the danger was very real. The Lucier family emerged alive but not unscathed, their spirit intact even as they navigated a deeply segregated society. And one child of the family left dead, likely as collateral damage for blurring the lines of social boundaries with white friendships and an era of war for civil liberties.

The Civil Rights Era
The Civil Rights Era, spanning the 1950s and 1960s, was a time of intense struggle and activism aimed at dismantling racial segregation and discrimination in the United States. It was a period when African Americans, particularly in the South, faced institutionalized racism through Jim Crow laws, which enforced segregation in public spaces, schools, and workplaces. This era was defined by landmark events such as the Montgomery Bus Boycott, the Selma to Montgomery marches, and the efforts of leaders like Dr. Martin Luther King Jr., Rosa Parks, and John Lewis. For African Americans living in rural Georgia, the fight for equality was deeply personal, as systemic oppression touched every aspect of their daily lives. The Lucier family's story is a reflection of this struggle, this pain, and life-long remembrance of events that altered the lives of all who witnessed.

Survival in the Face of Adversity
Ethel Lucier worked tirelessly to protect and provide for her children during this tumultuous time. Living in what was colloquially known as "Dark Town," they witnessed firsthand the pervasive injustices of segregation. Despite these challenges, she was determined to give her children an opportunity for a better life. Many of their children- the grandchildren of Henry T. and Ethel- eventually left Georgia, heading west to California in search of freedom and prosperity that their hometowns could not provide.

Before leaving, however, they faced profound struggles. Segregated schools under Jim Crow laws were severely underfunded, offering outdated textbooks and minimal resources. Schools like Pike County Consolidated High School in Concord served all Black students in the county from the 1950s until its closure in 1969. The school stood as both an educational and community center, where students received not only an education but also a sense of solidarity. Yet, systemic barriers often delayed or prevented graduation for many Black students, including members of the Lucier family.

Pike County Consolidated School Gymnasium, Hilltop, Concord, Georgia

Geneva Woods-Mangham

The Protest of 1969

For decades, African- American students, from kindergarten to 12th grade, were housed under the single roof of Pike County Consolidated in Concord, Georgia. In 1969, the closure of Pike County Consolidated High School marked a pivotal moment in the community's history. With integration of the all-white Pike County High School, the school district's superintendent decided not to renew the contracts of Black teachers and administrators, including the beloved principal, D.F. Glover. Geneva Mangham Woods was the only black teacher that was reinstated. In response, on a sunsplashed Monday morning in April 1969, Sammy Starks led as the seniors began a silent walkout. Many students from other grades followed. Police and sheriff's deputies followed them. The students, including members of the Lucier family, led a courageous march from Hilltop, 7 miles, to the Pike County Courthouse in Zebulon. They were met by state troopers, helicopters, and the Atlanta news media. As punishment for their defiance, the students were denied their graduation ceremony and diplomas.

This injustice was not forgotten. In 2018, nearly 50 years later, with the help of Geneva Mangham Woods, the students of Pike County Consolidated High School's Class of 1969 were finally recognized. They received their diplomas during a special ceremony, along with an apology and a resolution from the Board of Education. It was a bittersweet moment of redemption for those who had fought so hard for their rights.

Samuel Starks and Dorothy Reid among other graduates from the Class of 1969 move their tassels from left to right during the graduation ceremony nearly 50 years after their last days of school at Pike County Consolidated High School, at the Pike County Auditorium in Zebulon on Saturday, March 3, 2018. Fifty-six years ago, the students at Pike County Consolidated High School, an all-black institution, emptied into the street to protest the way desegregation was being handled in their community. By way of punishment, the entire Class of 1969 was barred from graduation.

Acts of Courage

The Lucier family's involvement in the Civil Rights Movement extended beyond the classroom. Shirley Starks was jailed twice for her activism. During her first imprisonment, she and others sang through the night to keep Sheriff J. Astor Riggins awake, a small act of resistance that symbolized their unyielding spirit. She was jailed for marching to Pike County High School after meeting with prominent leaders of the Southern Christian Leadership Conference (SCLC), including Ralph David Abernathy, Hosea Williams, Andrew Young, A.D. King, C.T. Biven, Willie Bolton, and John Lewis. Her second imprisonment stemmed from a false accusation of inciting a riot, based on a note written by a classmate. She would be kicked out of Pike County Schools and forced to register in Griffin School District. Only to graduate 2 years post schedule in 1973.

When J. Astor was sheriff

J. Astor Riggins was elected sheriff in 1953. He lived with his wife in a white frame house that served as the sheriff's department and county jail until it was torn down in 1975 to make way for the new building. His wife did the cooking for the prisoners. For 11 years, Riggins worked alone, without deputies, the only law in Pike County. He hired his brother in 1964.

Sitting in an empty grand jury room on the second floor of the courthouse, under the whirring blades of an antiquated ceiling fan, Riggins takes a break from campaigning to discuss his candidacy. He says he hits the road each morning at 7 a.m. in his 1972 Ford pickup, and that he has already visited 50 percent of the households in Pike County.

Riggins was at the center of controversy in November, 1969, when he jailed five black high school students — ages 15 through 17 — who had been accused by the principal of disrupting classes. The arrests followed a six month school boycott by blacks that had ended the previous month.

Systemic Changes for All

"I am somebody" a phrase that became a rallying cry during the Civil Rights Movement, emphasizing self-worth and dignity for Black Americans. Other family members, including Sammy Starks, Dorothy Reid, David Reid, and Mike Starks stood in solidarity with Shirley, marching alongside each other in protest of the unjust integration of 1969 in Pike County, Georgia. Their fight was for the right of every student in their family and the generations to come. Their fight was for every Black household in Pike County, Georgia, Unknowingly, they were shaping the future of education in Pike County, challenging systemic inequities and paving the way for lasting change. By 1970, The children of the Lucier's had become a generation of fighters, trailblazers, and change-makers; the pioneers of the Bayard Rustin quote, "We need, in every community, a group of angelic troublemakers."

Pike High graduates 73

Pike County High School presented diplomas to 73 seniors last night at graduation exercises. The honor students were in charge of the program.

Those receiving diplomas are:

Edward Terrel Adams, Lula Mae Alred, Donna Lynn Bell, Barbara Jean Blackmon, Cathy Jean Boswell, Andrew Lee Bradshaw, Terry Dale Breier, Willie Larry Britton, Willie Therone Bunkley, Gwendolyn Dianne Burden, Pinkney Wynton Carter, Susan Joan Chandler, Randolph Alton Clark, Ulysses Clark.

Willie Fred Colquitt, Bobbie Oneita David, Melvin Davis, Charles Robert Dunn, Danny Flemister, Mollie Ann Flemister, Sandra Ford, Richard Lee Fordham, Carol Annette Foster, Debra Elaine French, Gloria Sue Garner, David Eugene Hamilton, David Wesley Heard, Michael Lee Henderson, Deborah Jane Hilley.

Betty Ann Hollis, Steve Marvin Huckaby, Larry Hutcherson, Audie Elmo Ingram, Richard Mac Keneipp, David Lamar, Loretta Leaks, Marcia Lee, Johnny Keith Legg, Mary Joyce Lucas, Mary Delois Lucier, Robert Michael Mallory, Dennis Eugene McDaniel, Carol Milby, Pamela Yvette Mills.

Lannie Milner, Danny William Nelms, Deborah Louise Owens, Stephen Ray Parks, Elder Pate, Sandra Joan Patton, James Kelvin Pennington, Eddie Joe Perdue, Jack William Pilkenton, Jr., Wayne Lee Pilkenton, Vera Maxine Potts, Chrystal Powers, Michael Sandefur.

Edna Carol Scoggins, Donald Gary Shackelford, Lyndie Lou Sharpe, Barbara Jean Shelton, Linda Gail Smith, Robert Therone Smith, Richard Michael Angelo Starks, Shirley Diane Starks, Dorothy Evelyn Tucker, Marilyn Tucker, Robin Sue Walker, John Horace Wellmaker, Lena Mae Williams, Mary Jean Williamson, William Rodney Willis, Mary Ruth Wright.

Pike County Integration
During the 1960s, schools across the South, including those in Georgia, began the process of desegregation following the Brown v. Board of Education decision in 1954 and the Civil Rights Act of 1964. In Pike County, like many rural areas in Georgia, integration was a gradual process and often met with resistance.

Pinkey Lucier was one of the first ten Black students to integrate Pike County High School. Lydia Starks, was a part of the first kindergarten class to attend Pike County Elementary's desegregated schools, marking yet another milestone in the family's journey. They both faced daily hostility as trailblazers in the desegregation of education.

 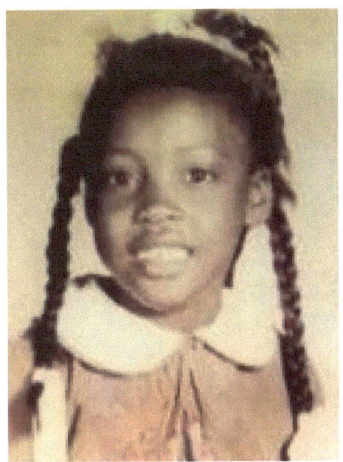

Pinkey Lucier & Lydia "Lisa" Starks

Historical Context of School Integration in Pike County
Segregation Era: Prior to the 1960s, schools in Georgia, including those in Pike County, were racially segregated due to Jim Crow laws. Black students attended separate schools, often with fewer resources than their white counterparts.

Brown v. Board of Education (1954):
The U.S. Supreme Court ruled that racial segregation in public schools was unconstitutional. However, many Southern states, including Georgia, resisted desegregation for years.

Civil Rights Act of 1964: This federal legislation mandated the desegregation of public schools and other facilities, accelerating the integration process.

Integration in Georgia: In Georgia, widespread school integration began in the late 1960s and early 1970s, as federal courts enforced desegregation orders. Many rural counties, including Pike County, were slower to integrate compared to urban areas like Atlanta.

"I am somebody. I may be poor, but I am somebody. I may be on welfare, but I am somebody. I may be uneducated, but I am somebody. I must be respected, protected, never rejected."
-Reverend Jesse Jackson

The Esteemed 6th Generation Scholars

Darlene Lucier O'Baner
- North Carolina Theological Seminary
  Griffin, Georgia

Pinkey Lucier
- Albany State University
  Albany, Georgia

Vanessa Lucier
- Albany State University
  Albany, Georgia

Carol Lucier Mobley
- Albany State University
  Albany, Georgia

Patricia Lucier Collier
- Griffin Technical College
  Griffin, Georgia

Samuel Starks
- Southern Crescent Technical College
  Griffin, Georgia

Faithe Houston Lyons
- Ohio State University
  Columbus, Ohio

Robert Starks Jr.
- Fort Valley State University
  Fort Valley, Georgia

Shirley Starks Ali
- North Carolina Theological Seminary
  Griffin, Georgia

Christopher Starks
- Chabot College
  Hayward, California

- San Francisco State
  San Francisco, California

Kathy Starks
- Atlanta Dental Institute
  Atlanta, Georgia

Leonardo Lucier
- Texas Southern University
  Houston, Texas

Carlon Lucier Taylor
- Savannah State University
  Savannah, Georgia

Zandra D. Lucier
- Southern Technology
  Marietta, Georgia

- Texas Southern University
  Houston, Texas

Vincent R. Lucier
- University of Georgia
  Athens, Georgia

Scott D. Lucier
- National-Louis University
  University of Phoenix

Marc Lucier
- Norfolk State University
  Norfolk, Virginia

Richard Calvin
- University of Southern California
  Los Angeles, California

- Washington State University
  Pullman, Washington

The Distinguished 6th Generation Business Owners

Ali, Shirley Starks- Educator and Entrepreneur. Event planner and caterer. Founder of Shirbaby in Griffin, Georgia.

Calvin, Richard- Athlete and National Football League (NFL) running back. Richard was drafted in 1988 by the Denver Broncos and later played for the Los Angeles Rams until 1991. Founding Partner of FireStarter Media Group

Collier, Patricia Starks- A community leader and the first Black Voter Registrar of Pike County, Georgia. She helped to register residents in voter desert areas of the county and gained recognition from many state leaders, including praise from Andrew Jackson Young.

Houston-Lyons, Faithe- (Deceased) Educator and retired elementary school teacher for the Columbus, Ohio Public School System.

Lucier, Don, William Jr., and Lacey- Musicians and original founding members of the Dynamic Gospel Flames, a famous gospel, live performing and recording music group in Griffin, Georgia.

Lucier, Leonardo Sr.- Entrepreneur and tax accountant. Founder of Tax King Pro and Lucier Tax & Financial Services, a personal tax and accounting firm in Atlanta, Georgia.

Lucier, Pinkey- Educator and retired elementary school teacher for Griffin-Spalding County School District.

Marshall, Jesse- (Deceased) Entrepreneur. Founded Marshall's Transfer, a transport and moving company in Griffin, Georgia, currently run and operated by his children. He also founded a car detailing company that serviced residents in the 4th Ward district and surrounding areas in Griffin, Georgia.

Mobley, Carol Lucier- Entrepreneur and Restaurateur. Founded the family's first restaurant, Taste and See Takeout Cafe, located at 320 South Cedar Ave, South Pittsburg, TN 37380.

Oliver, Rochelle- Minister of Music and entrepreneur. Praise and worship leader in Rochester, New York, and founder of an ecommerce party services and gifting company specializing in t-shirts, special gifts, blinged-out footwear, baby gift boxes, and party favors via Facebook @RochelleOliver

Reid, David- Entrepreneur and retired videographer and photographer. Celebrated for his unwavering media presence and connections to various events throughout Griffin, Ga and its neighboring counties. The First genealogist of the family, preserving the family's heritage by creating a 90's reunion video for the Lucier-Lindsey families, which documented the genealogical journey of the Lucier family

Starks, Christopher- Entrepreneur who founded the first Black-owned produce market in Griffin, Georgia, with locations on Solomon Street and the flagship site on Taylor Street. The flagship location gained recognition by being featured in the Oscar-winning film "Fried Green Tomatoes." He developed one of the first mobile food trucks selling fresh fruits and vegetables in the country, visiting low-income neighborhoods to provide access to healthy food and increase the equity of nutrition. Additionally, he made history as the first Black utility locator in the state of Georgia, establishing Signal Utilities, to prevent damage to underground infrastructure, ensure safety, and legal compliance of underground utilities.

Starks, Joe Scott- Entrepreneur and certified driver. Owner-operator of a trucking business.

Starks, Richard- Certified driver and owner-operator of a trucking business.

Starks, Robert Jr.- Entrepreneur. Founded Starks Locating Company, a utility locating company that services residential and businesses in Georgia.

Starks, Samuel- Entrepreneur. Former cosmetologist and salon owner. Currently a certified driver and owner-operator of a trucking business.

Starks, Russell- Community leader and certified state umpire. Multi-disciplined sports coach with over 30 years of experience in Griffin and surrounding Georgia counties.

Smith, Cynthia Starks- Minister and theologian in Georgia.

Lucier, Scott- Defense and information technologist and consultant. Founder and principal of SETT Inc., a provider of information technology services that focuses on delivering innovative solutions in Anne Arundel County, Maryland.

The Legacy of Education
Education was a cornerstone of the Lucier family's plan of ascent. Despite the systemic inequalities of the time, they were forced to come up with solutions that would elevate their current standings. Pike County Consolidated High School, like many Black schools in the rural South, operated with limited resources but served as a beacon of hope. The Rosenwald Schools, funded by philanthropist Julius Rosenwald, were another critical resource, providing educational opportunities for African American students across the South, including Georgia. These schools symbolized the community's determination to overcome adversity through education- even on limited to no funding needed to appropriate change.

County	School (Bold Faced Equals Extant Historic Resource)	Budget Year	No. Teachers	Total Cost in Dollars	Rosenwald Fund Contribution in Dollars
Pierce	Patterson School	1928-1929	2	3,050	500
Pike	Central School	Tuskegee Period	1	996	300
Pike	**Concord School**	1929-1930	2	2,650	500
Pike	Zebulon School	1926-1927	2	3,000	700
Polk	Cherokee School	1926-1927	2	2,715	700

Rosenwald Schools Funding Rubric

A Legacy Continued
The grandchildren of Henry T. and Ethel Lucier went on to raise children of their own, many of whom had the privilege of meeting their great-grandmother Ethel before her passing in 1985. Today, these great-grandchildren, and now the second great-grandchildren of Henry T. and Ethel- carry forward the family's legacy. They are tasked with preserving the truth, power, and fight for freedom that has defined the Lucier family for generations.

This story is a testament to the courage and determination of a family that has faced and risen above adversity at every turn. From the struggles of segregation and the Civil Rights Era to the challenges of modern-day inequality, the Lucier family's journey serves as a powerful reminder of the enduring fight for justice and equality. Today, the grandchildren of Henry T. and Ethel are comprised of College Graduates, Certified Tradesmen, Military Vets, Teachers and Educators, Photographers, Entrepreneurs, Cosmetologists, Accountants, Musicians, Preachers, Restauranters, Realtors, Coaches, Consultants and so many other things.

Every generation and branch of the family that followed has achieved the unimaginable- rising to new heights, breaking barriers, and seizing opportunities that once seemed out of reach. And it is all because of the unwavering dedication of the parents and grandparents who came before them- those who endured unthinkable hardships, made sacrifices, and held onto faith when opportunities were scarce. Their resilience paved the way, and their legacy continues to inspire us to press forward- giving us the will to be powerfully free.

LUCIER

MILITARY
SERVICE

LUCIER

LUCIER

Notable U.S. Military War Service
1918- 1971

	Henry T. Lucier	**Bennie Lucier**	**Willie Lucier**	**Eddie Lucear**
Rank	Private	Private	Private	Private First Class
Branch	United States Army	United States Army	United States Army	United States Army
Specialty	Infantry Division	Infantry Division	Infantry Division	Infantry Division
Era	WWI	WWI	WWI	WWII
Enlistment Date	3 Apr 1918	3 Apr 1918	5 Aug 1918	13 Mar 1943
Discharge Date	17 Jan 1919	24 Feb 1919	6 Oct 1918	3 December 1945
Years Served	9 months	11 months	2 months	2 years, 9 months
Insignia	Private chevron	Private chevron	Private chevron	PFC chevron
Hometown	Williamson, Georgia	Williamson, Georgia	Williamson, Georgia	Concord, Georgia

  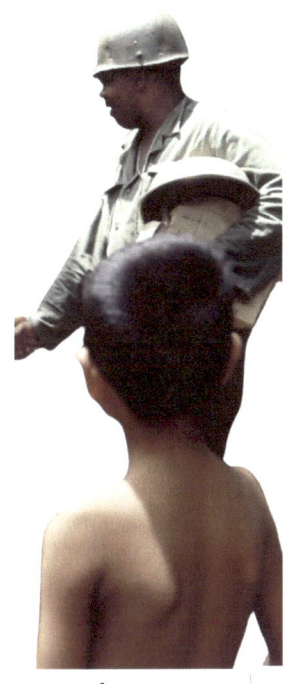

	James Henry Lucier	**William Lucier**	**Josiah Lucier**
Rank	Staff Sergeant	Private	Hospital Corpsman Second Class (HM2)
Branch	United States Army	United States Army	United States Navy
Specialty	Corps of Engineers	Signal Corps	Field Medical Service Technician
Era	WWII, Korean War	WWII	Vietnam War
Enlistment Date	28 Mar 1941	13 Mar 1943	8 Jun 1954
Discharge Date	31 Mar 1961	3 December 1945	26 Jan 1971
Years Served	20 years	2 years, 9 months	16 years, 8 months
Insignia			
Hometown	Williamson, Georgia	Williamson, Georgia	Williamson, Georgia

U.S. Military Veterans & Active Duty
1918- present

Mohib Ali- Air Force
Troyius Brown- Marines
Zadiah Freeman- Navy
Eddie Lucear Sr.- Army
Benjamin Lucier- Army
Hermon Lucier Jr.- Marines
Henry T. Lucier- Army
Mary Lucier- Army (Ret.)
Will Lucier- Army
Willie Lucier- Army
Scott Lucier- Navy (Ret.)
Marc Lucier- Marines
Anthony Marshall- Army
Darlene O'Baner- Army (Ret.)
O' Kendrick Reid- Army (Ret.)
Grant Reid- Army
Cory Simmons- Air Force (Ret.)
Christopher Starks- Army
Richard Starks- Army
Samuel Starks- Navy
Scott Starks- Navy
Willie Starks Jr.- Navy
Willie Starks Sr.- Army
Dominique Taylor- Army (Active)

LUCIER

THE APPENDIX

LUCIER

LUCIER

SURNAME EVOLUTION CHART

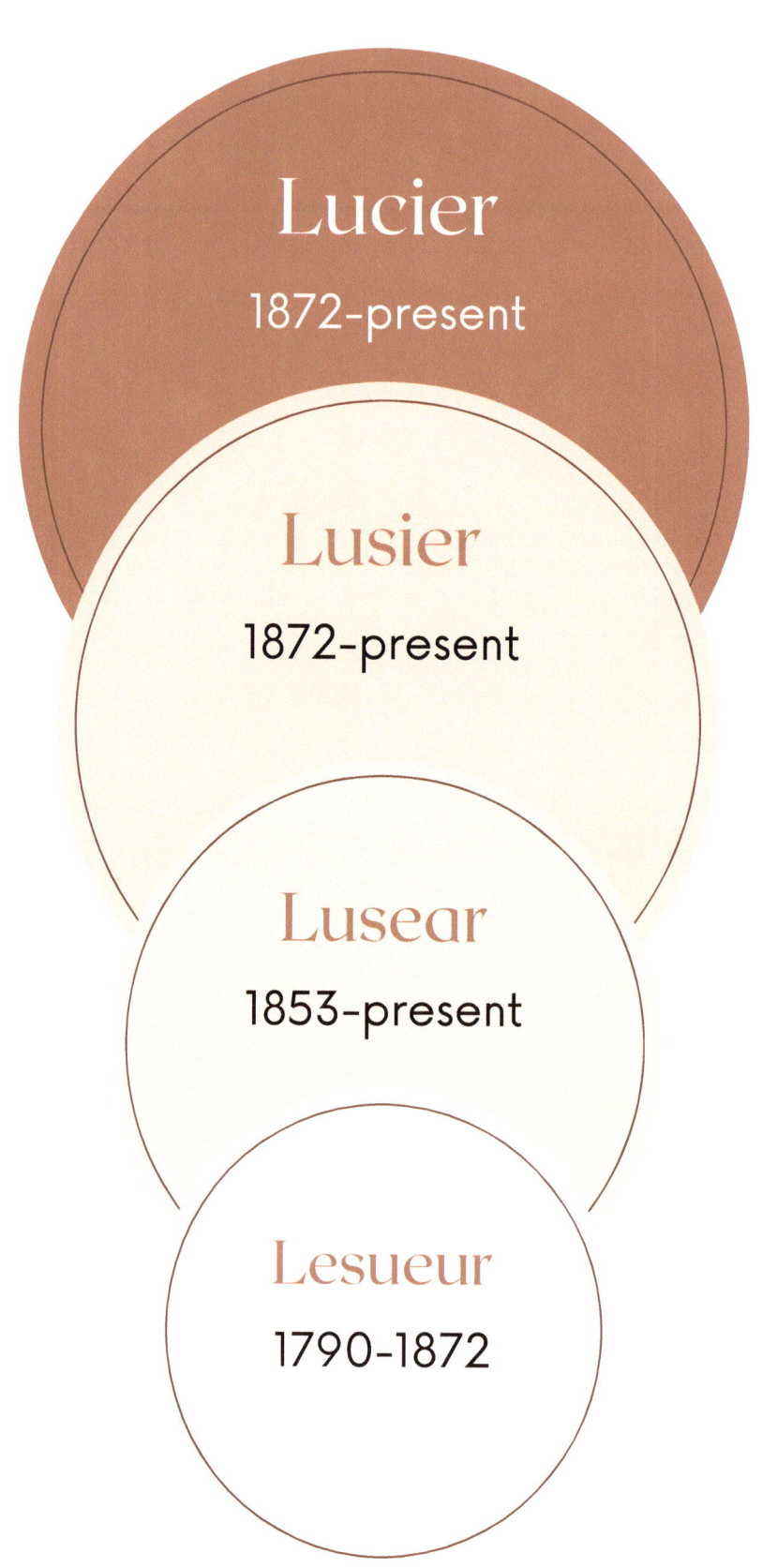

GENERATIONAL MAP | 2025

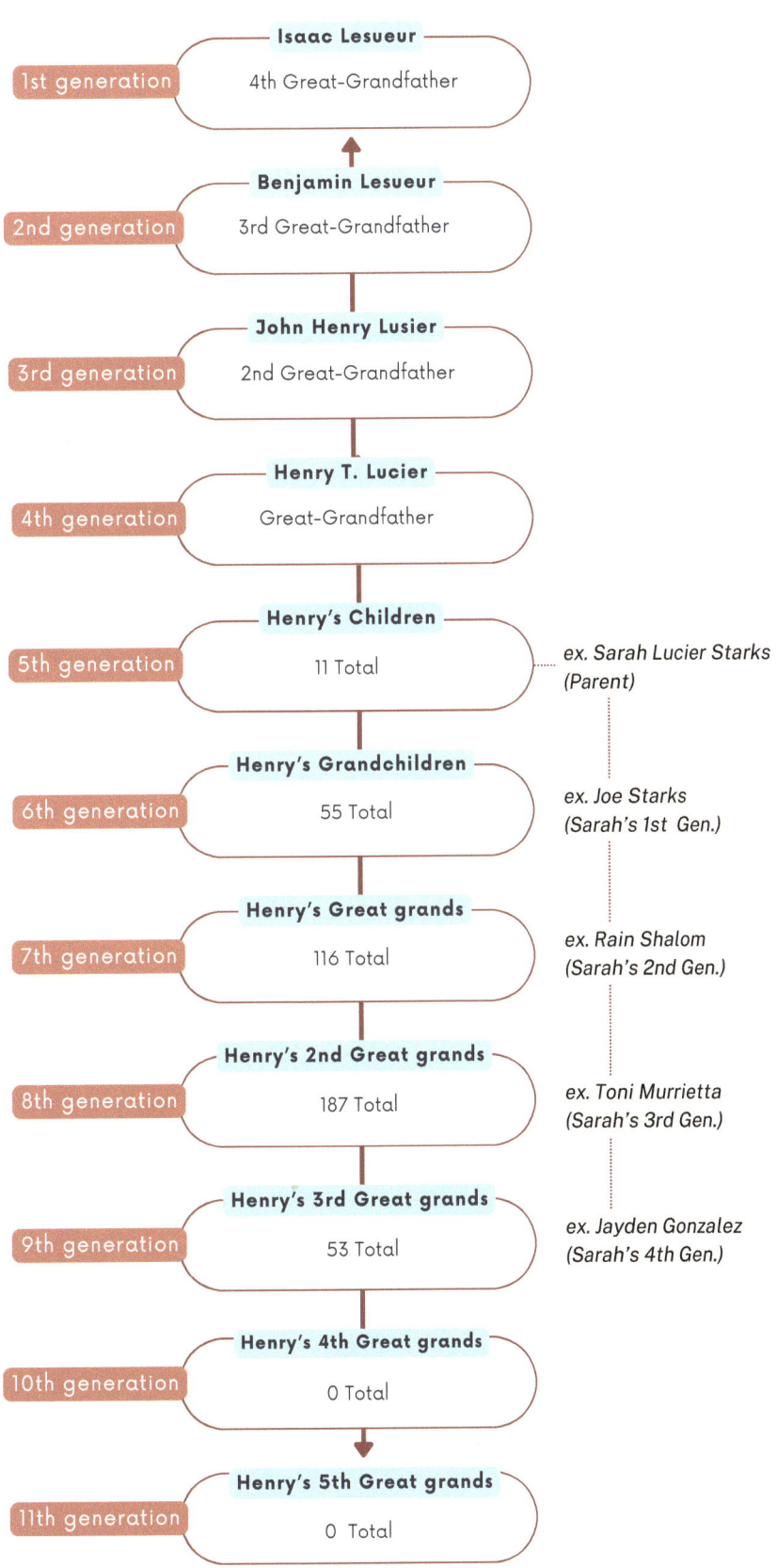

GEORGIA MIGRATION PATTERNS

The Lucier family has a long history of migrating from Georgia to various states, with many returning as older adults, unwell, or after passing away to be laid to rest alongside family. The first documented migration from Georgia dates back to 1938. To this day, numerous descendants have chosen to weave their lives across the tapestry of the United States, finding new homes far from their ancestral roots. This map illustrates the locales where Henry T.'s descendants dwell, yet it captures but a mere glimpse of the many migrations that have unfolded from Georgia.

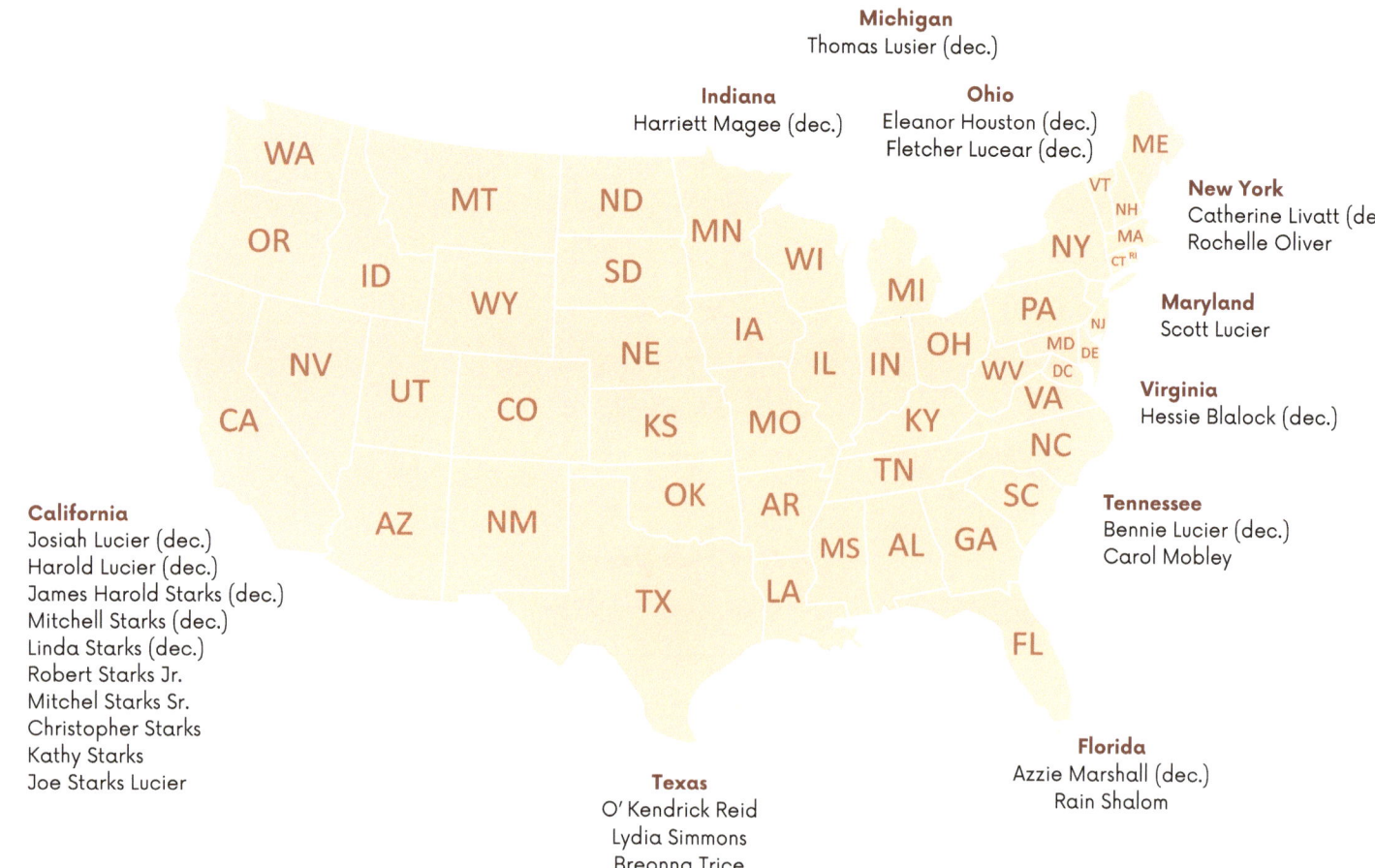

Michigan
Thomas Lusier (dec.)

Indiana
Harriett Magee (dec.)

Ohio
Eleanor Houston (dec.)
Fletcher Lucear (dec.)

New York
Catherine Livatt (dec.)
Rochelle Oliver

Maryland
Scott Lucier

Virginia
Hessie Blalock (dec.)

Tennessee
Bennie Lucier (dec.)
Carol Mobley

California
Josiah Lucier (dec.)
Harold Lucier (dec.)
James Harold Starks (dec.)
Mitchell Starks (dec.)
Linda Starks (dec.)
Robert Starks Jr.
Mitchel Starks Sr.
Christopher Starks
Kathy Starks
Joe Starks Lucier

Texas
O' Kendrick Reid
Lydia Simmons
Breonna Trice

Florida
Azzie Marshall (dec.)
Rain Shalom

GLOSSARY

Abolishment: The act of formally ending a system, practice, or institution, such as slavery.
Ancestry: Lineage or descent from a particular ancestor or group of ancestors.
Antebellum: Refers to the period before the U.S. Civil War, particularly in the Southern United States.
Battalions: Military units consisting of a headquarters and two or more companies or similar units.
Biological: Relating to the natural processes and characteristics of living organisms.
Camp Greenleaf: A U.S. Army training camp during World War I, located at Fort Oglethorpe, Georgia, primarily for medical personnel.
Camp Hancock: A U.S. Army training camp during World War I, located in Augusta, Georgia.
Camp Wheeler: A U.S. Army training camp during World War I, located near Macon, Georgia.
Cavalry: A military unit mounted on horseback or, in modern times, using armored vehicles.
Chiefdom: A form of political organization in which a chief holds power over a group of communities.
Colloquial: Language used in ordinary or informal conversation rather than formal writing.
Colonial: Relating to the period when a country establishes control over another territory.
Commodified: The process of turning something into a commodity for economic gain.
Confederacy: The Confederate States of America, formed by Southern states that seceded from the Union during the U.S. Civil War.
Confederate supporter: An individual who supported the Confederate States of America during the U.S. Civil War.
Confederate sympathizer: Someone who expressed sympathy or support for the Confederate cause.
Connotations: Ideas or feelings that a word invokes beyond its literal meaning.
Constitution: A set of fundamental principles or established precedents according to which a state or organization is governed.
Creek Muscogee Indian: A member of the Muscogee (Creek) Nation, a Native American tribe.
Crohn's disease: A chronic inflammatory condition of the gastrointestinal tract.
Debt peonage: A system where laborers are bound to work to pay off a debt, often under exploitative conditions.
Demarcate: To set boundaries or limits.
Derogatory: Expressing a low opinion or disrespect.
Descendants: Individuals who are the offspring of a particular ancestor or group.
Dialects: Regional or social varieties of a language distinguished by pronunciation, grammar, or vocabulary.
Discrepancy: A lack of consistency or agreement between facts or figures.
Draft Registration: The process of enrolling individuals for compulsory military service.
Emancipation: The act of freeing someone from legal, social, or political restrictions, particularly the freeing of enslaved people.
Enslavement: The state of being owned and controlled by another person as property.
Freedman: A formerly enslaved person who has been emancipated.

Freedman's tax list: A record of taxes paid by freedmen after emancipation.
Freemason: A member of the Free and Accepted Masons, a fraternal organization.
Fort McPherson: A U.S. Army base located in Georgia, active during various conflicts.
Fort Oglethorpe: A U.S. Army base in Georgia, used during World War I.
Fort Screven: A former U.S. Army fort located on Tybee Island, Georgia.
Genealogical: Relating to the study of family ancestry and history.
Great Migration: The mass movement of African Americans from the rural South to the urban North during the 20th century.
Hierarchies: Systems of organization in which people or groups are ranked above one another.
Immigrant: A person who moves to a new country to settle permanently.
Indigenous: Originating or occurring naturally in a particular place; native.
Infantry: Soldiers who fight on foot.
Jim Crow era: The period of racial segregation and discrimination in the United States, particularly in the South, from the late 19th to mid-20th century.
Ku Klux Klan: A white supremacist organization founded in the U.S. after the Civil War.
Legitimation: The process of making something lawful or valid.
Loyalty oath: A pledge of allegiance to a government or cause.
Lusitania: A British ocean liner whose sinking by a German submarine in 1915 influenced U.S. entry into World War I.
Marginalization: The process of making a group or individual less important or relegating them to a powerless position.
Maritime disaster: A catastrophic event occurring at sea, often involving the loss of ships or lives.
Mattaponi: A Native American tribe located in Virginia.
Meuse-Argonne Offensive: A major part of the final Allied offensive in World War I.
Mico: A term used among some Native American tribes to refer to a chief or leader.
Migration: The movement of people from one place to another, often for settlement.
Militia District: A local administrative division for organizing military or civil defense.
Minstrel shows: A form of entertainment featuring racist caricatures of African Americans, popular in the 19th and early 20th centuries.
Mulatto: A historical term for a person of mixed white and Black ancestry.
Muscogee: A Native American people originally from the southeastern United States.
Namesake: A person or thing named after another.
Native American: A member of any of the Indigenous peoples of the Americas.
Oconee: A Native American tribe originally from the southeastern United States.
Ogeechee: A river in Georgia, also associated with a Native American tribe.
Pamunkey: A Native American tribe located in Virginia.

GLOSSARY

Patriotic: Having or expressing devotion to one's country.
Plantations: Large agricultural estates, historically reliant on enslaved labor.
Port of Embarkation: A harbor or city where troops or goods are loaded onto ships for transport.
Post-emancipation: The period following the abolition of slavery.
Posthumously: Occurring after a person's death.
Racial ambiguity: The state of having an unclear or mixed racial identity.
Rappahannock: A Native American tribe located in Virginia.
Reconstruction Era: The period following the U.S. Civil War, focused on rebuilding the South and integrating formerly enslaved people into society.
Reconstruction Oath: A pledge required of Southerners to regain political rights after the Civil War.
Selective Draft Act on May 18, 1917: U.S. legislation authorizing the conscription of men for World War I.
Sharecropping: A system where landowners allow tenants to use their land in exchange for a share of the crops produced.
Sharecroppers: Farmers who work on land owned by others in exchange for a share of the crops.
Shenandoah Valley: A region in Virginia and West Virginia, historically significant in U.S. history.
Shortline operator: A person or company that operates a short railroad line.
Slaveholder: A person who owned enslaved individuals.
Southern Christian Leadership Conference: A civil rights organization founded in 1957, closely associated with Dr. Martin Luther King Jr.
Stereotypes: Oversimplified and generalized beliefs about a particular group of people.
Stigma: A mark of disgrace associated with a particular circumstance, quality, or person.
Systemic inequities: Structural inequalities embedded within societal institutions.
Systemic oppression: Institutionalized mistreatment of a group within society.
Taxation: The imposition of compulsory levies on individuals or entities by a government.
Tenant farming: A system where farmers rent land and pay the landowner with a portion of their crops.
The Great Depression: A severe worldwide economic downturn during the 1930s.
The Great Migration: The mass movement of African Americans from the rural South to the urban North during the 20th century.
The Union: The United States, particularly during the Civil War, referring to the Northern states.
Treaty of Versailles: The peace treaty that ended World War I in 1919.
Trench warfare: A type of combat in which opposing troops fight from trenches facing each other.
Tribal council: A governing body within a Native American tribe.
U.S. Civil War: The conflict between the Northern and Southern states from 1861 to 1865.

Veterans Day: A U.S. holiday honoring military veterans, observed on November 11.
Whig settlements: Communities established by supporters of the Whig political party in the 19th century.
White supremacy: The belief in the superiority of white people over other racial groups.

FAMILY BIRTH & DEATH

Name	Date of Birth	Date of Death

FAMILY BIRTH & DEATH

Name	Date of Birth	Date of Death

FAMILY BIRTH & DEATH

Name	Date of Birth	Date of Death

FAMILY BIRTH & DEATH

Name	Date of Birth	Date of Death

FAMILY MARRIAGE

Groom	Bride	Date	Location

FAMILY MARRIAGE

Groom	Bride	Date	Location

FAMILY MARRIAGE

Groom	Bride	Date	Location

FAMILY MARRIAGE

Groom	Bride	Date	Location

Meet The Author & Chief Editor

LYDIA SIMMONS

Lydia Simmons, a maternal health pioneer, researcher, and entrepreneur, is the founder of Motherocity Health, an AI-powered platform transforming postpartum care worldwide. A four-time patent and trademark holder, she has authored medical journals and analyses across four continents, earning recognition for excellence in innovation from Forbes, Ebony, Essence, Newsweek, TechCrunch, Bustle, and WELL+GOOD.

Named after her aunt, Lydia Starks- who was tragically killed in 1970 during the Civil Rights Movement- she grew up immersed in family stories that, after 40 years, sparked a dedicated effort to document the Lucier family lineage dating back to the 1700s. In a powerful continuation of family tradition, she later named her first daughter after her beloved aunt, a pattern she discovered had repeated throughout generations. Through meticulous research, she weaves together a compelling account that preserves their legacy for the future.

May the Lord watch between Me and Thee,
while we are absent, one from another.
Amen.

LUCIER

© 2025 Lydia Simmons.
Lucier Family Story | Vol. I
Austin, Texas
ISBN: 979-8-218-62831-4

All rights reserved. No portion of this book may be reproduced or transmitted in any form, mechanically, electronically, or by any means including photocopying, without written permission from the publisher, except for brief quotations in reviews.

Cover design by Lourdes Simmons, Cruz Simmons
Interior design by Lourdes Simmons, Cruz Simmons

Printed in United States

www.ingramcontent.com/pod-product-compliance
Lightning Source LLC
Chambersburg PA
CBHW041417010526
44107CB00016B/1205